ZEN Horses

Drawing Amazing Zen Doodle Horses

By Jane McKenty

Table of Contents

Disclaimer

While all attempts have been made to verify the information provided in this book, the author does assume any responsibility for errors, omissions, or contrary interpretations of the subject matter contained within. The information provided in this book is for educational and entertainment purposes only. The reader is responsible for his or her own actions and the author does not accept any responsibilities for any liabilities or damages, real or perceived, resulting from the use of this information.

The trademarks that are used are without any consent, and the publication of the trademark is without permission or backing by the trademark owner. All trademarks and brands within this book are for clarifying purposes only and are the owned by the owners themselves, not affiliated with this document.

Introduction

If you were looking for a complete guide to Zen Doodle, **"ZEN Horses-A Complete Guide to Master Horse Drawings in Zen Doodle"** is the right book for you. This book is written in a comprehensive manner so that even a layman can understand the concept and the basics of Zen Doodle. Zen Doodle is a relatively new concept in the field of art. Even though many people subconsciously draw the Zen Doodle patterns, still they do not know about the exact name for this genre. In this book, we have tried to explore the concept of Zen Doodle to a great depth.

You will not face any difficulty in learning Zen Doodle drawings through this book. Moreover, there are several illustrations of complete Zen Doodle designs in the form of horse. Step by step drawings let you complete the sketch in no time. We have also tried to teach you how you can take inspiration from different sources.

The concept of Zen Doodle is altogether a very easy one.

You do not have to be a professional artist to try your hands on this genre of art. Just a pen and a sheet of paper are needed to get started. Once you get the hang of basic patterns, you can modify any picture into a Zen Doodle design. Just get started with this book and you will get the confidence of exploring new patterns all by yourself.

Enjoy drawing!

Section 1

Chapter 1 - What is Zen Doodle?

As you know, the concept of Zen asserts that you can attain enlightenment through meditation. Also, you must be aware of the term "doodle". Just the way you doodle anything on a piece of paper, you can Zen Doodle as well. Humans have been doodling since the Stone Age, when they made patterns in sand using a twig. Hence the term Zen Doodle is a combination of two words "Zen+Doodle". Zen Doodle is just like meditation. When you enjoy drawing random patterns on paper without giving it much thought, you are zendoodling.

Some kind of elusiveness exists about this concept because different people have different approach towards Zen Doodle. Just like different people meditate differently; they make drawings of Zen Doodle differently. There are no strict rules for these drawings. That is why; many concepts and definitions have originated for Zen Doodle.

However, for the sake of keeping it simple, we will define it for you. Zen Doodle is a drawing which you make in your leisure time, without paying much attention. You can be occupied in other things while making these drawings. But, you cannot do the same in other genres of art.

A Zen Doodle drawing becomes a beautiful artwork when you become detached from other things and focus on intricate doodling. The "inventors" of Zen Doodle place special emphasis on focused attention. And the fixed formats for the drawings are used for Zendoodling. Ideally, a 3.5 inch square is used to create the drawings. Earlier it used to be mindless drawing, but now has become much more sophisticated. The use of proper formulas, methods, composition and patterns gives a consistent look to the Zen Doodle drawings.

You must have doodled on the margins of your notebooks in school. They were the baby steps for Zen Doodle. Now if you refine those drawings with formulaic methods, you can create beautiful Zen Doodle drawings. You should avoid thinking about other things while you do the sketching.

Chapter 2 – Zen Doodle as Meditation

If you doodle in your free time, it can be actually therapeutic for your brain in the form of meditation. You can also compare Zen Doodle with Yoga. The way you feel relaxed after a session of Yoga, you feel highly contented after making a few drawings of Zen Doodle.

Art forms of all kinds are said to have therapeutic effects on your mind, body and soul. Even if these art forms are not legally certified, still people do it for relaxation. There are a few things around us which have meditative effects on our mind. And we do not need any certifications or approvals to heal ourselves. For example, pottery is a form of art, which many people start as a part of their relaxing and detoxification sessions, but they end up becoming a master in pottery.

Similarly, you can say the same for Zen Doodle. You do not need to think much before sitting down to make drawings. Just take a piece of paper and a pen; and start filling up a sketch with any kind of patterns your mind can think of.

There are many examples of people who say that they reach a stage of trance while making Zen Doodle drawings. There are others who play the new age music or Trance music while drawing. Doodling Zen patterns can be a soothing break from the stress of your daily life. Zen Doodle can also be called as a non-verbal conversation of proportions and pattern; which leads you to open the doors of insights which you thought were locked before.

When you draw Zen Doodle, you can enter a state of meditation and you experience a free flow of intuition. When your mind is calmed by this state of relaxation, you can get answers to your worries without any hindrance from your worries or expectations. Inspirations and ideas take a new turn with Zen Doodle. Since you do not have to follow any specific rules, you become aware of new patterns and the structures underlying them.

You can call Zen Doodle as means and metaphor for flourishing your intuitive awareness. By doing this, you are allowing your creativity to move in unexpected directions. When you revisit your drawings later, you will realize that you were definitely in some other state of mind when you drew the Zen Doodle illustrations. The drawings are like a trail of your dreams, which can remind you of your state of trance even after years.

Doodling can be just a fun activity, but if you sit down with proper set of mind, you can create something, which you never expected. And the good news is that you do not have to be a professional artist for mastering Zen Doodle. The patterns of this genre are such that anyone can try their hands on it.

Chapter 3 - How Did It Start?

There is no specific date known for the beginning of Zen Doodle. But, there are folks who tried to doodle with some meditative patterns. Gradually, this genre of art took its roots and is a much talked about topic on the Internet. Many creators of Zen Doodle say that they experience feelings of timelessness and freedom while drawing Zen Doodle.

The system came to the fore gradually after the genre got its followers. Many books and articles have been written in the last few years. You can find ample of drawings around you if you start looking for Zen Doodle followers. And not just followers, there are many people who do not know about this genre. But, when they look at these drawings, they can relate to them. Many collectors of art are also interested in buying these drawings and paintings. Now, after so many years of its advent, Zen Doodle has established itself as a genre of art, which is included in the mainstream art.

Chapter 4 - About Horses in Art and Zen Doodle Horses

Horses are one of the favorite subjects of artists. They are not very easy to draw but not very difficult either. The plus point about drawing horses is that you can explore hundreds of things while drawing. It is such a beautiful creation of God that it has become a darling theme for artists and photographers alike. You must have seen magazine covers, posters, calendars, T-shirts prints, drawing tutorials, and many more such things. The movements and expressions of horse give ample of material to the budding artists to practice their drawing. In this book, we have also taken few drawings of horses and tried to explore them with Zen Doodle techniques.

There is a plethora of illustrations of horses over the Internet. After you read this book, you can take the help of any of those illustrations to improvise your skills. Moreover, we would suggest that you start small at the drawings. Take any size of the sheet you want and start practicing. Set genuine and achievable targets and try to achieve them. Do not get de-motivated if are not able to achieve your targets as and when you had expected. There are millions of examples of people who get successful after hundreds of trials.

In this book, we have explored different patterns to draw horses. The designs are so alluring that you will get mesmerized once you get habitual to the patterns. Horses have been depicted in art throughout the works of historian artists in history. It was majorly because they used to be a major means of transport in ancient and medieval times. Modern day artworks that depict horses are related to horse races, cowboy paintings, etc.

Genres of Art Depicting Horses

There have been different genres of art that have depicted horses.

Military Art

Military art often expresses horses in battle, the horse driven chariots, horse archers, etc. Such artifacts appear all over the pages of history.

During the medieval period, there were many examples of horses being portrayed in the paintings like knights riding horses and cavalry battles. Artists who made such paintings include **Albrecht Dürer** and **Paolo Uccello**. Interestingly, **Sir Alfred Munnings** was assigned the post of a "war artist" to paint the World War I. Munnings painted both the Canadian Forestry Corps, which was stationed in France and Canadian Cavalry Brigade. Famous as **Lady Butler**, Elizabeth Thompson made a lasting impression through her military art.

Horse Racing

The impressionist era of art coincided with the gradual development of horse racing in France. The impressionist artists were greatly inspired by thoroughbred racing in 19th century. **Manet** depicted the excitement of horse racing in his paintings. **Degas** depicted the moments before the race started. He was also fascinated by the photographs of **Muybridge**, showing horses in action. He made the paintings of those photographs, of which he took references in chalk and pencil. Artists like Alfred Munnings and George Stubbs have left behind a vast legacy of horse art, mainly focusing on horse racing.

Artists of 20th century like **John Skeaping** have made life size bronze sculptures of horse breeds like Brigadier Gerard and Hyperion. He also made many water color paintings of horses in action in races.

The American West

The tradition of native America, particularly the American West has many paintings based on equine or horses. Artists like **CM Russell** and **Fredric Remington** are well known for their horse paintings. Before the advent of photography, the artists were not able to portray the gait or manner of walking of the horses. Remington was one of the earliest artists who were able to portray the gait accurately. He also made a commercially successful bronze sculpture, Bronco Buster.

Modern Art

The most famous artist of the modern age, Pablo Picasso also incorporated horses in his art work. Some famous examples of horse paining by Picasso are Guernica, Boy Leading a Horse. Franz Marc, Deborah Butterfield and Susan Rothenberg also used horses as subjects in sculptures and paintings.

Hunting

It is a very common subject for artists who like to paint the equine. Horses have been used for hunting and wars from the ancient times. Artists like Lionel Edwards and Cecil Aldin are the famous examples of such artists.

Rural life/ Work life

Apart from bulls and cows, the use of horses for cart pulling, transportation was very common in the ancient times. They formed a major part of the rural life. Artists like Lucy Kemp Welch is very well known for her works of art depicting working horses as well as wild horses in the scenery.

Horses in History

Horses were depicted in the cave dwellings found in North Africa and Europe. This proves that horses have been used by humans for various purposes even before the recorded history. Many sites like Lascaux, Niaux, Vallon-ont-D'arc and some sites of France and Spain have depictions of rural life on their walls. Astonishingly, one-third of these paintings are of horses. Whatever was their inspiration to draw horses at such a scale, the fact is established that humans and horses shared an important relationship. As the time passed, horses were domesticated and the civilizations expanded.

Horses have been loved by man for various reasons. Not just because they were useful to man, they are fascinating creatures as well. Horse is a human friendly animal. They have been a partner of man in work, active participant in sports, a status symbol, a symbol of activeness, living essence.

We have mentioned this brief history about horses so that you can also take inspiration from various artist and paintings of horses. Drawing Zen Doodle horses can be easy as well as difficult at the same time. It depends upon how you perceive the subject. You can explore the genre of Zen Doodle in horses as main theme to a great extent. There is no limit to creativity. We have depicted relatively easier illustrations for you in this book. But, if you find these drawings easy, you can try and invent many more new patterns in the genre.

Chapter 5 - Applications of Zen Doodle

There can be hundreds of applications of Zen Doodle. We have listed some applications for you so that you can create your own Zen Doodle creations through various media.

Education

There can be many uses of Zen Doodle in various departments of education like:

- Coordination of eyes and hands
- Personal expression and creativity
- Handwriting improvement
- Problem solving
- Understanding of patterns of different cultures
- Focusing and concentration
- Confidence

Entertainment

You can hold art sessions particularly for Zen Doodle artist friends. Call some of your friends, hand over some Zen Doodle patterns to them and create some group paintings. You will be surprised to see the marvelous outcomes.

Gifts

You can create your own Zen Doodle cards and gift them to your friends and relatives on their special occasions like birthdays, anniversaries and many more.

Goodies

You can find many shops in the market which print the design or photograph of your choice on a T-shirt, coffee mug, cushion covers, pens, etc. You can get your designs printed on any of these goodies you want for yourself. You can also gift them to someone.

Therapy

There are many therapeutic uses of art forms. Zen Doodle can also be used for therapy of many incurable diseases, which require mental peace. Some of the clinical applications of Zen Doodle include:

- Improving self esteem

- Stress management

- Anger management

- Improved attention and concentration

- Addiction therapy

- Stroke recovery

Chapter 6 - Which Tools Should Be Used for Zen Doodle?

There are many tools available in the market, especially designed for Zen Doodle drawings. We have listed some of the essential tools which you can buy for creating masterpieces. But, we essentially suggest that you should just start with a pen and a paper. Then, you can gradually move towards other tools.

A pen

A micron black pen with a very fine tip is used for Zen Doodle drawings. You can buy different sizes of pen-tips to explore the designs. There are other options of lettering pens in market which you can give a try. You can also buy colored lettering pens if you are interested in colorful Zen Doodle drawings.

Drawing paper

You can use Bristol drawing paper for creating Zen Doodle drawings. You can also create the tiles of 4-5 square inches and practice different patterns on these tiles.

Tortillion

A tortillion is a smudge stick used to smudge various intricate portions of your drawings. You can use this tool once you learn drawing the designs perfectly. After that you can jump to the shading part.

Waterproof Ink

It is a very crucial part of your Zen Doodle kit. Waterproof ink is required so that if the paper becomes soggy due to weather conditions, your drawings remain intact. Even if you accidentally spill water over your creation, you still have chances of saving your drawing.

Colorless blender pen

It is used to lighten the ink and give special effects to your ink drawings. It is used to blend two colors. You can use this blender pen when you are creating Zen Doodle drawings in different colors. You can create subtle gradations with this amazing tool.

A pencil, sharpener and eraser

There are many designs which are complicated and require a rough draft before you make the final version. Thus, you would need a good quality light pencil, a sharpener and a high quality eraser. Do not make very dark impressions of pencil. Also, avoid using the eraser as much as possible. Keep the eraser just for emergency situations.

Section 2
Chapter 1 - Horse Drawing 1

By now, you must have learnt the basics of Zen Doodle. We will start drawing our first Zen Doodle drawing in the shape of the horse. In the coming chapters also, we will draw the horse only, but with different adaptations of Zen Doodle patterns.

Step 1

Draw the shape of a horse standing on its hind feet. If you are not comfortable in drawing it directly with a pen, you can draw it using a very light pencil first and then outline it with a pen. But, do not draw the embellishments with pencils. They have to be strictly drawn with pen only.

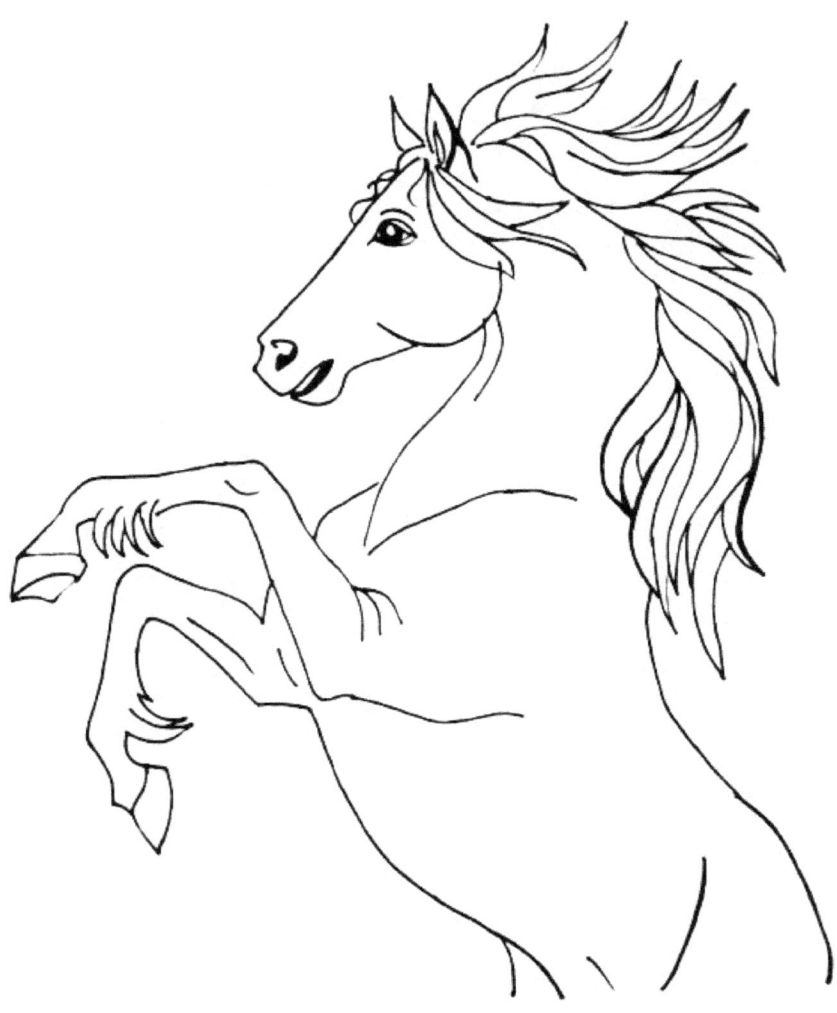

Step 2

Start filling the "mane" or the hair of the horse with different patterns of Zen Doodle. You can use zig-zag patterns, striping, dots, etc. to fill the mane.

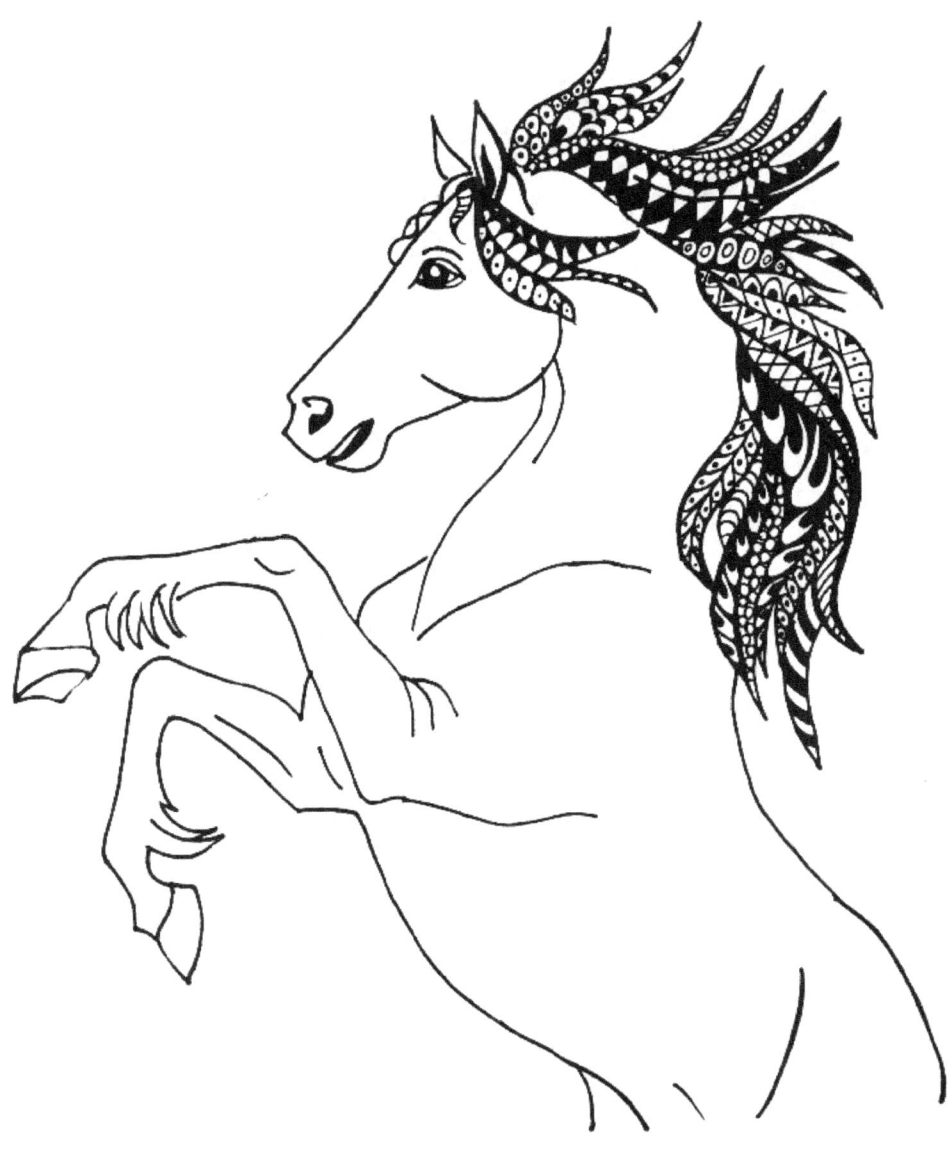

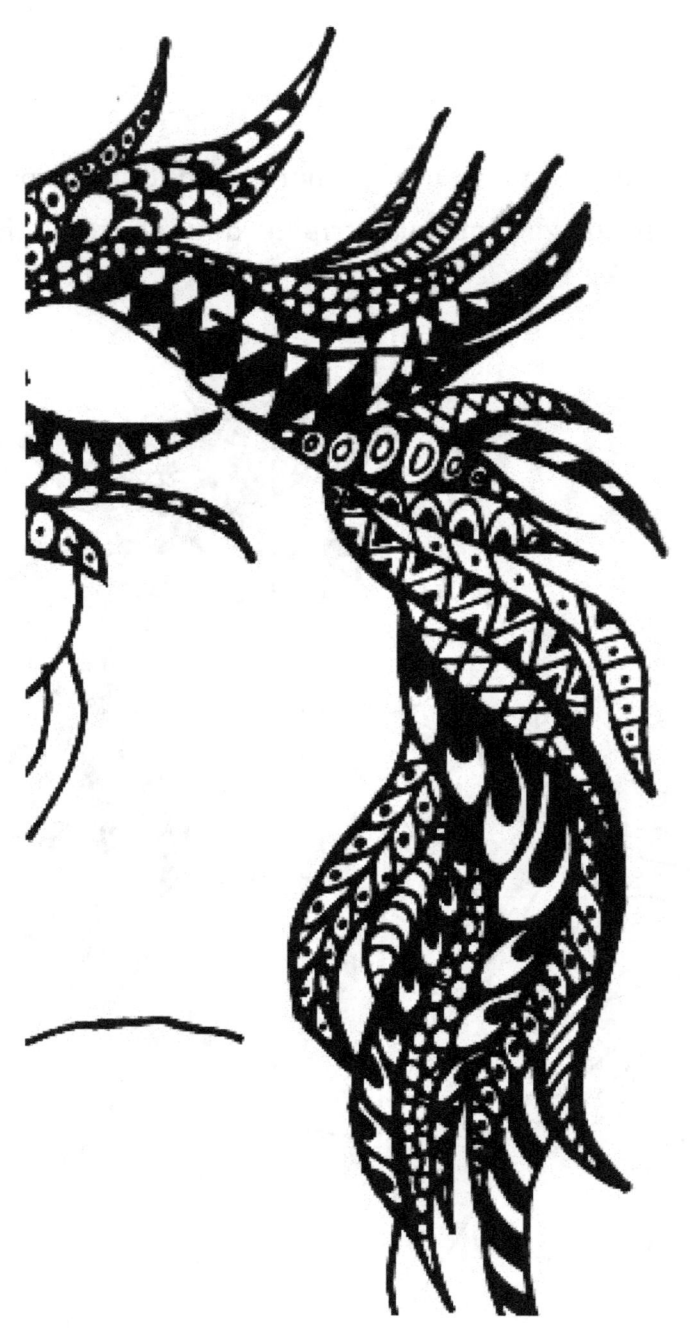

Step 3

Fill the neck with the starry pattern you can see in the illustration.

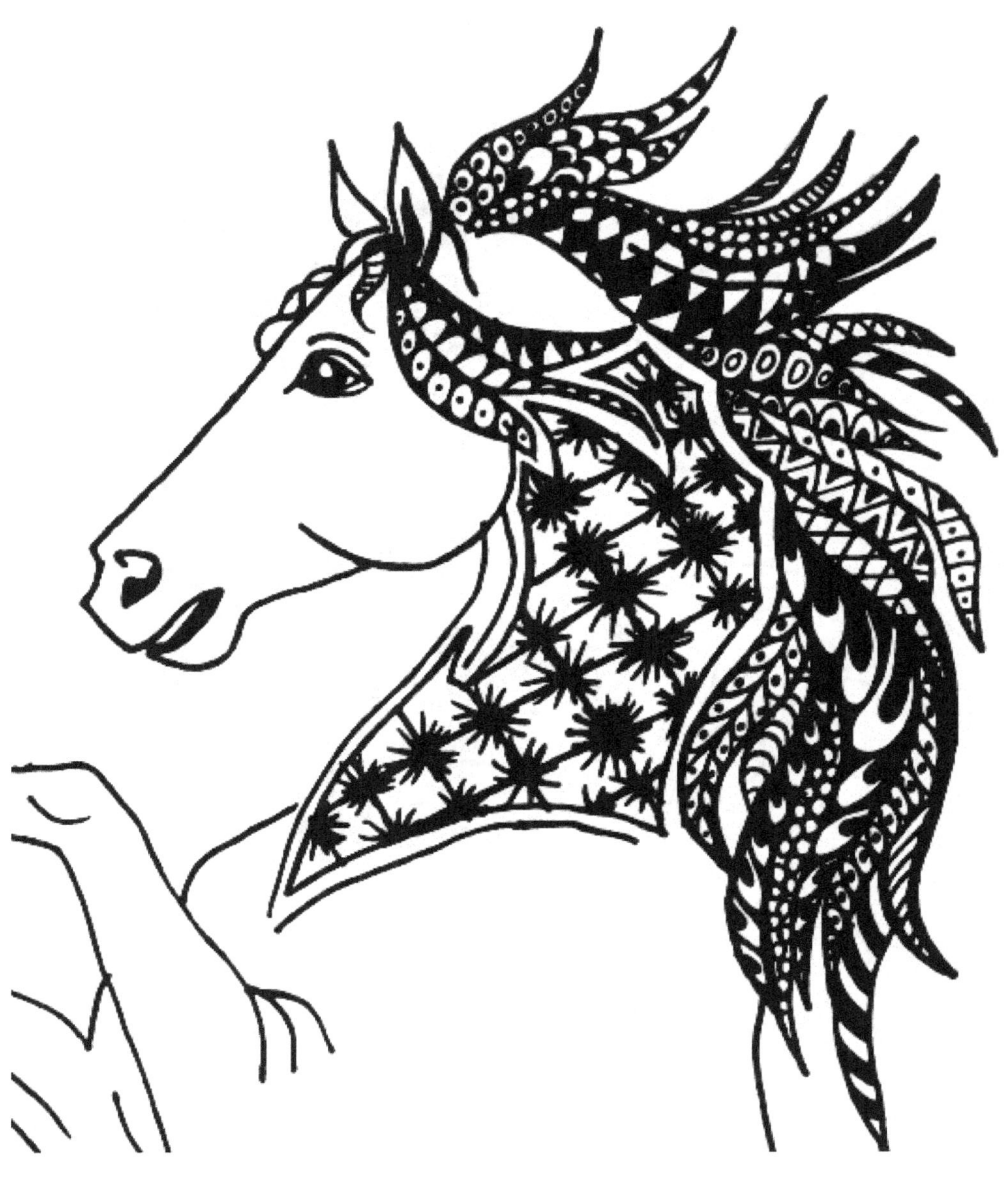

Step 4

Fill up the shoulder and elbow portion of the forearm with curved striping and the eye-like patterns.

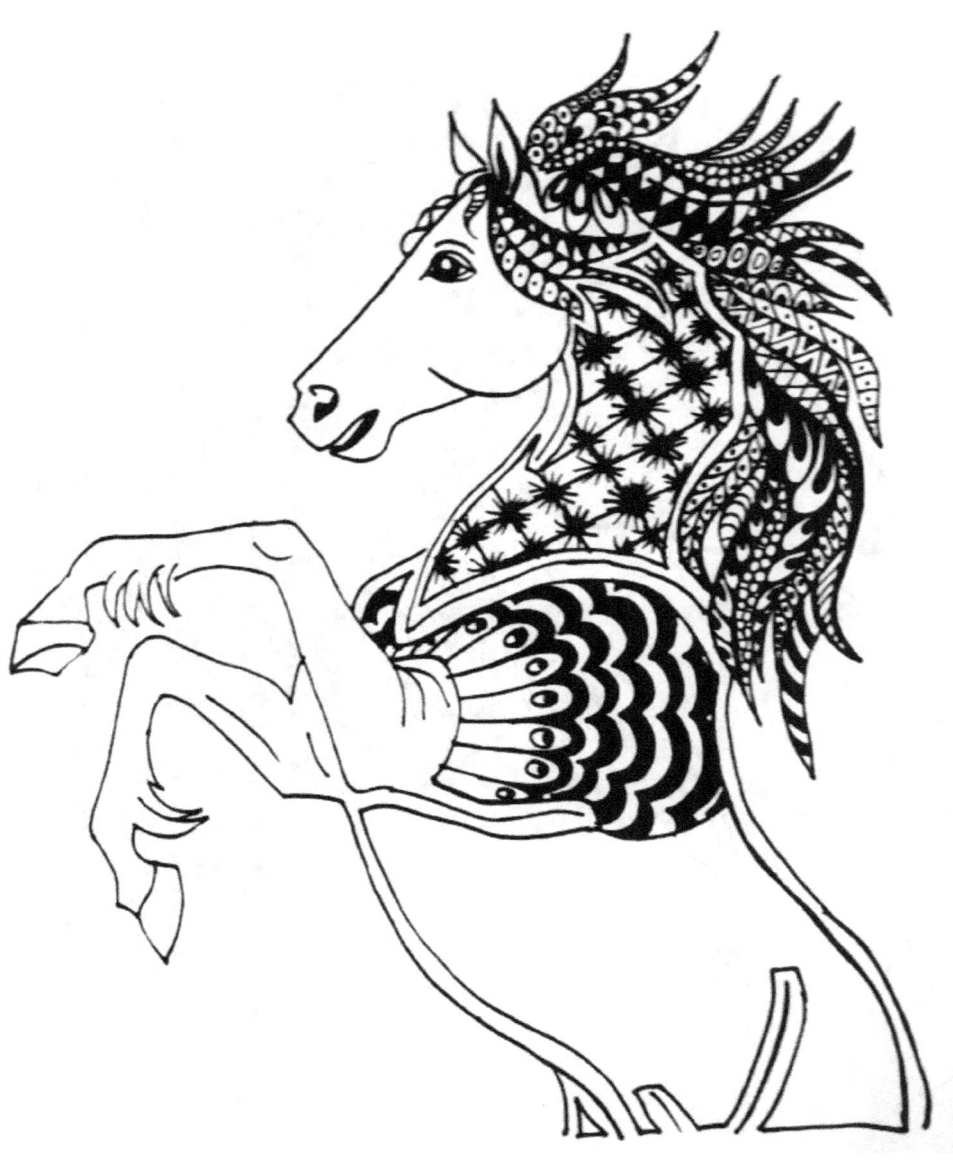

Step 5

Fill the rest of the girth or body of the horse with leaves filled with stripes or eye-like patterns.

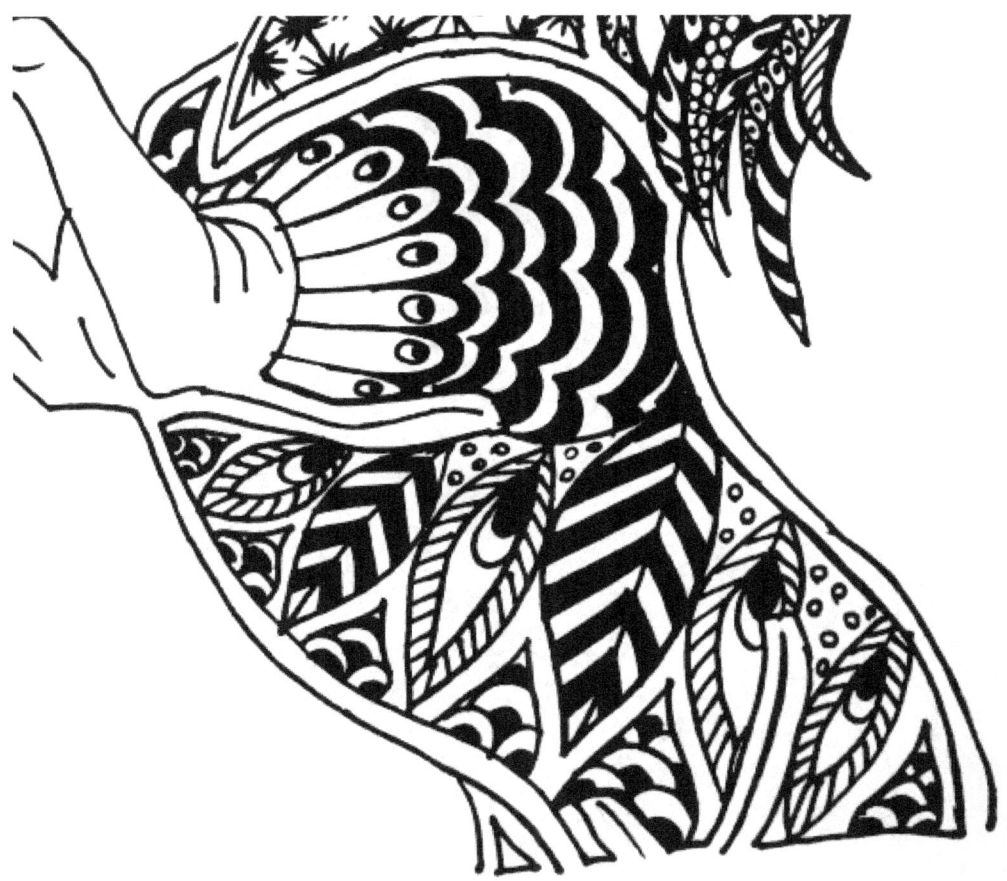

Step 6

Decorate the feet of the horse with embellishments. You can use spirals and filled semi-circle patterns.

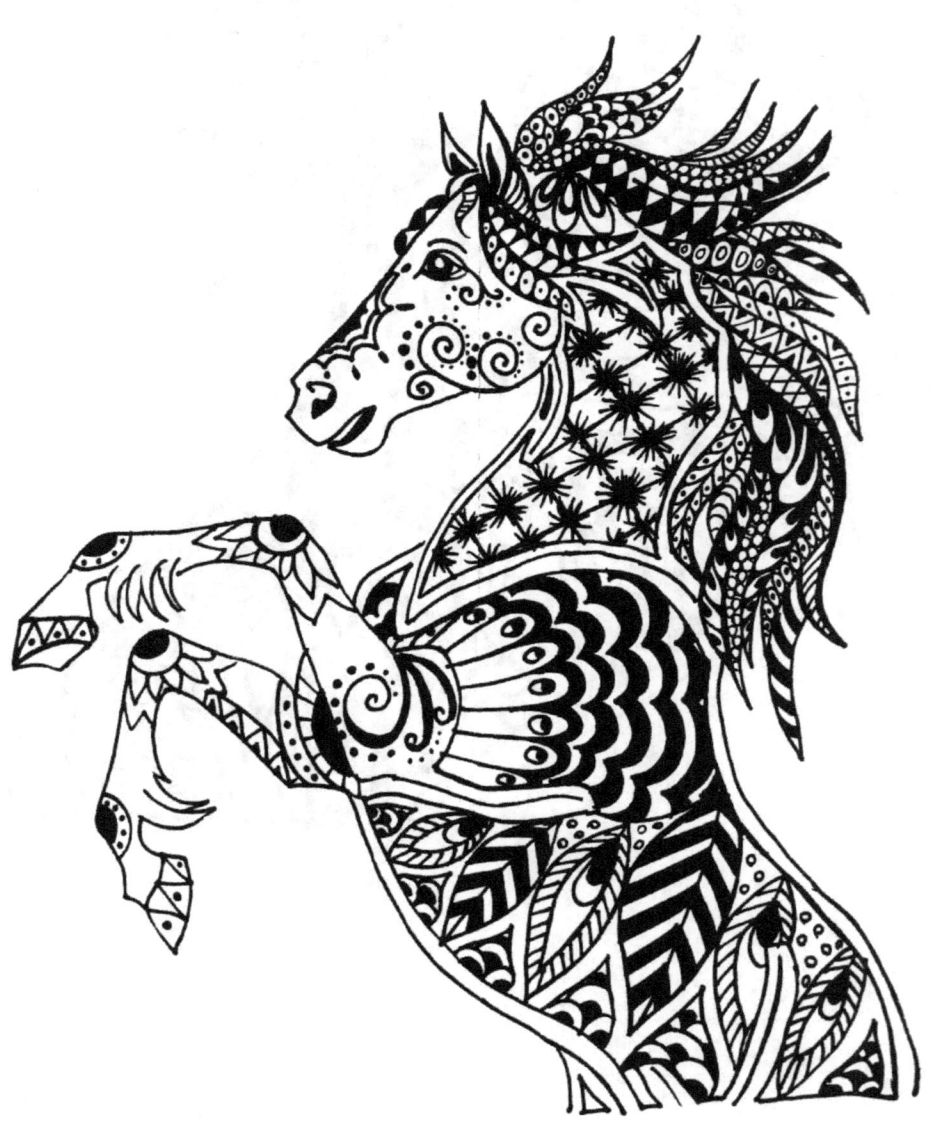

Chapter 2 - Horse Drawing 2

Step 1

Draw the basic shape of a horse. You do not have to stick to the traditional drawing of a running horse. You can use spirals or any curved lines while drawing the basic outline.

Similarly, the tail can be drawn using swirls.

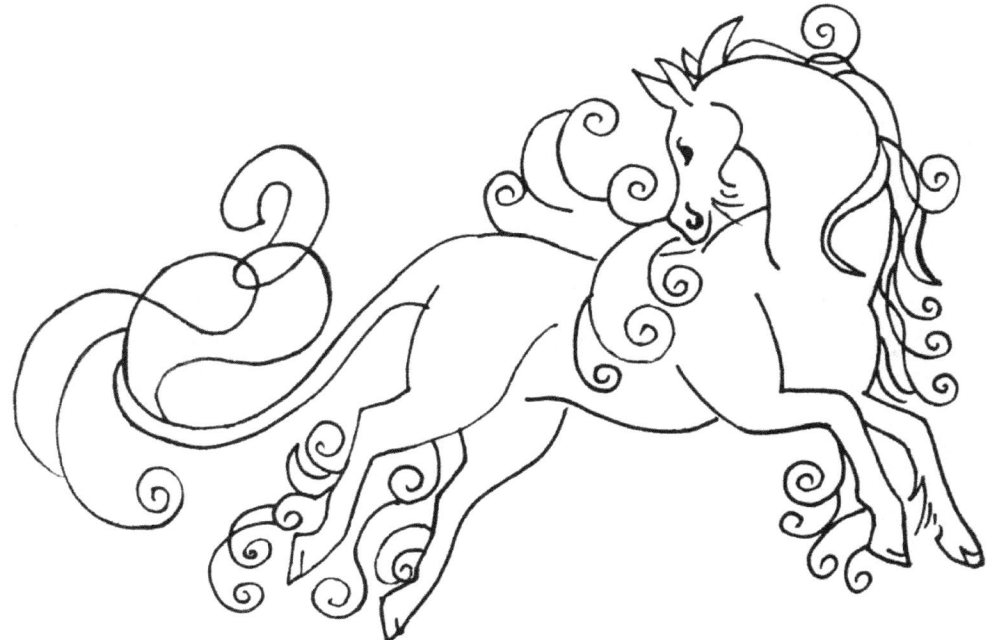

Step 2

Draw a few swirls in the drawing at the mane, top of the body and near the feet. The swirls should be bold at the stems.

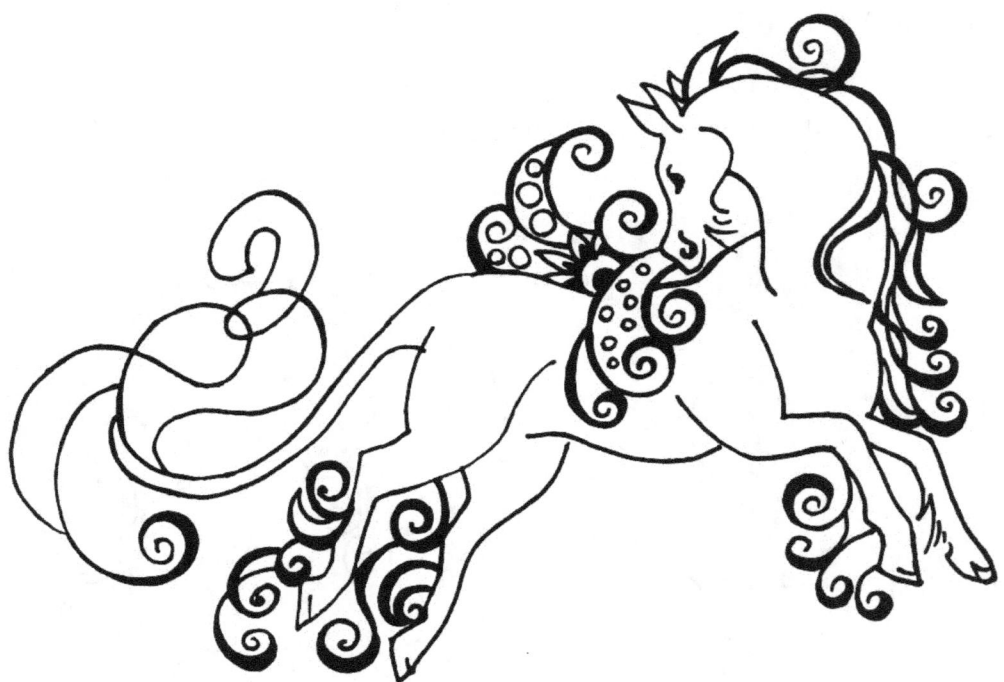

Step 3

Draw the swirls around the tail. Compose the swirls such that you can incorporate some more patterns in between them.

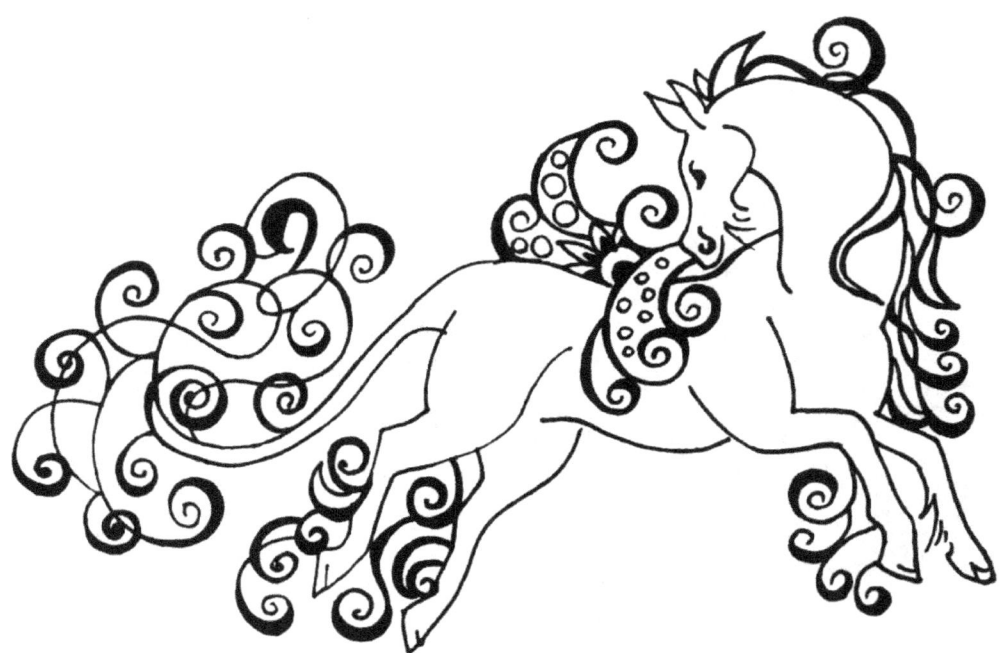

Step 4

Draw a spider web at the gaskin or the back of horse. Notice the strip of semi circles drawn in a beautiful pattern in the tail. Draw a different pattern in one of the hind legs to differentiate it from the other hind leg.

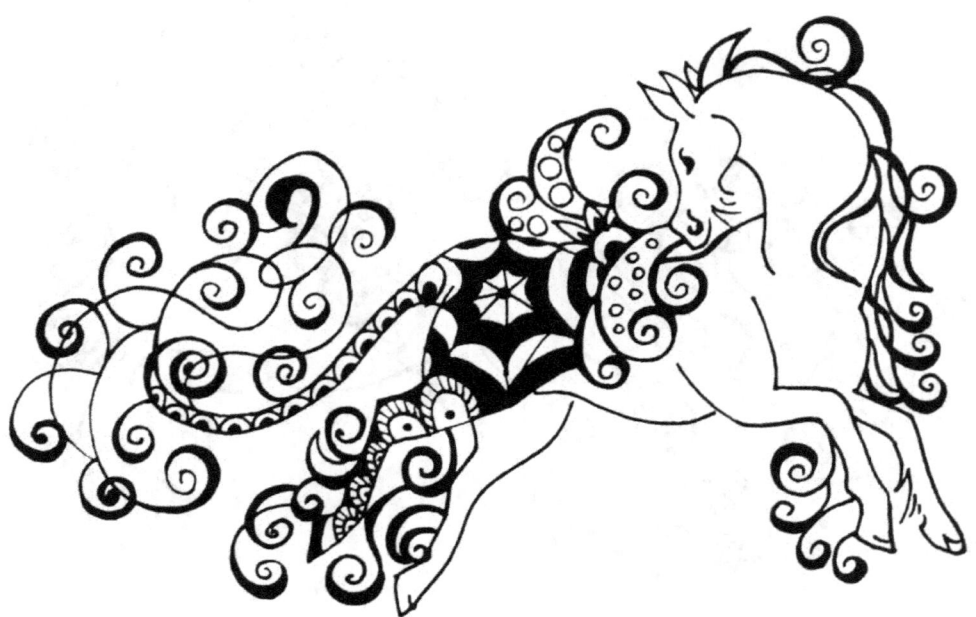

Step 5

Fill up the rest of the body of the horse with different patterns including circles, orbs, swirls, eye-like, spider webs, dots, etc.

The Zen Doodle running horse is complete.

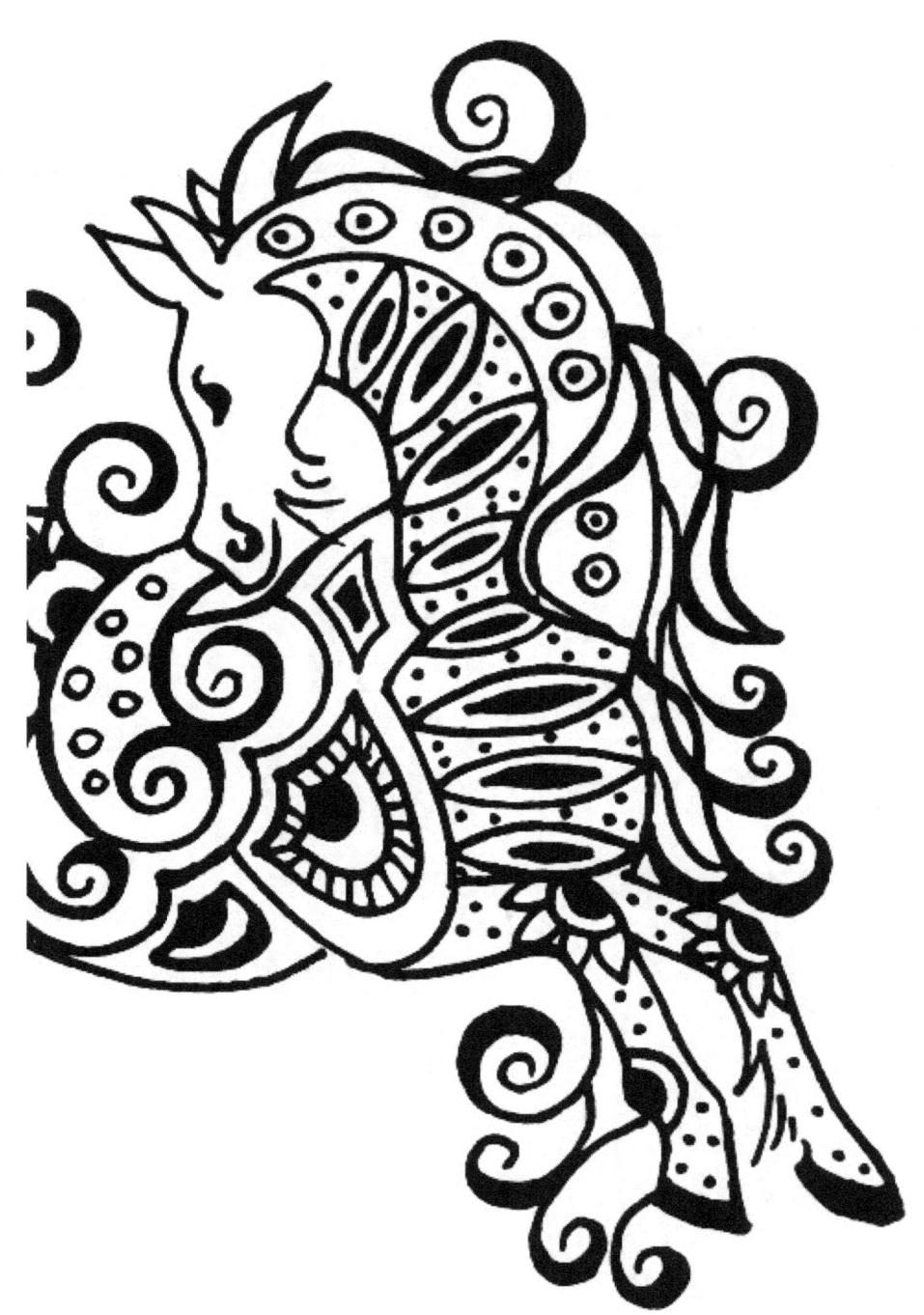

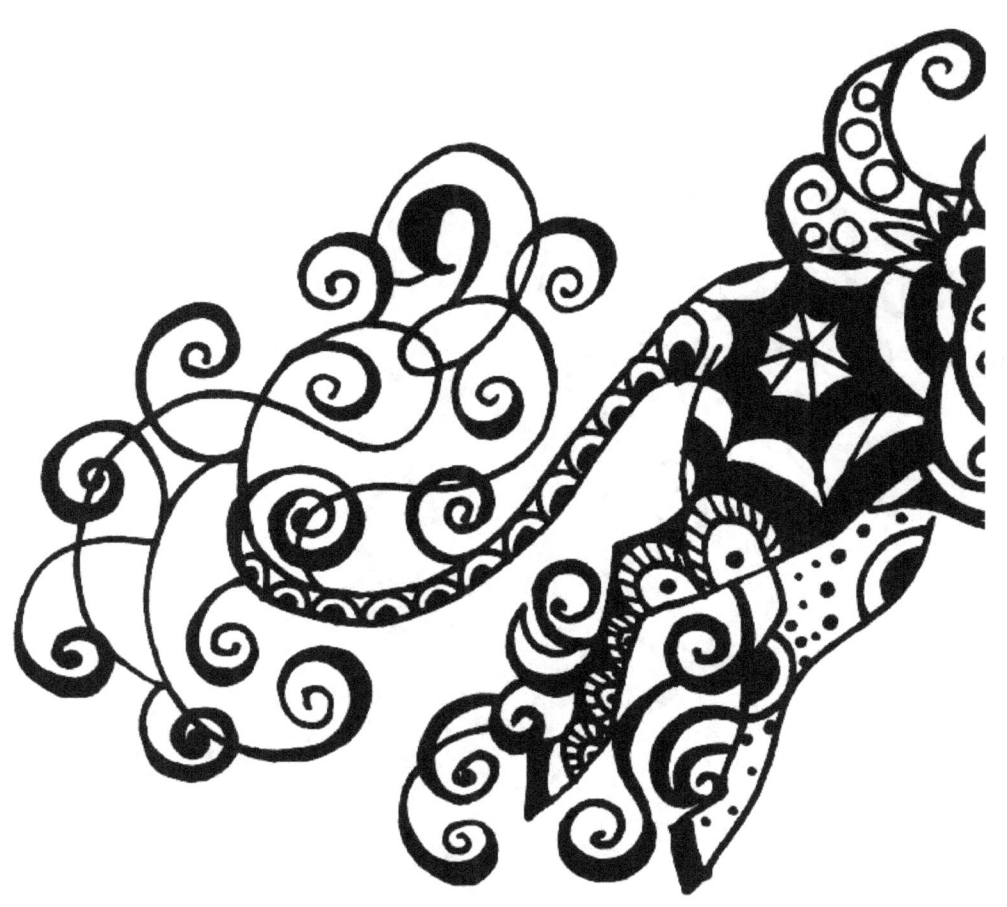

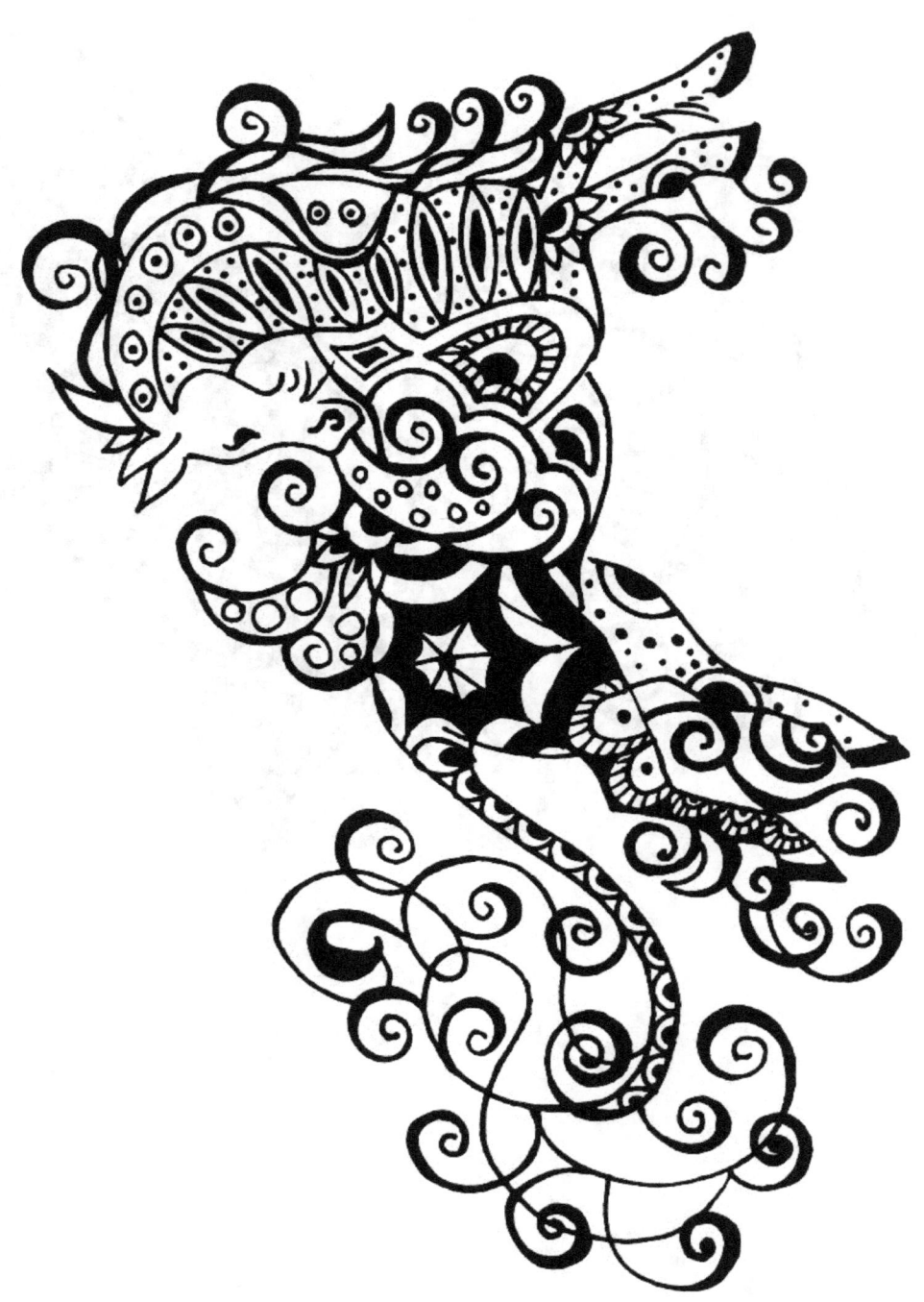

Chapter 3 - Horse Drawing 3

Step 1

Draw the basic outline of a horse standing on its hind legs. The drawing of this horse is similar to that of the horse in previous chapter. But, we will create the patterns in a different way in the body of the horse.

Draw the finishing ends of the mane and the tail carefully. The curved and pointed ends create the beauty of the Zen Doodle animal.

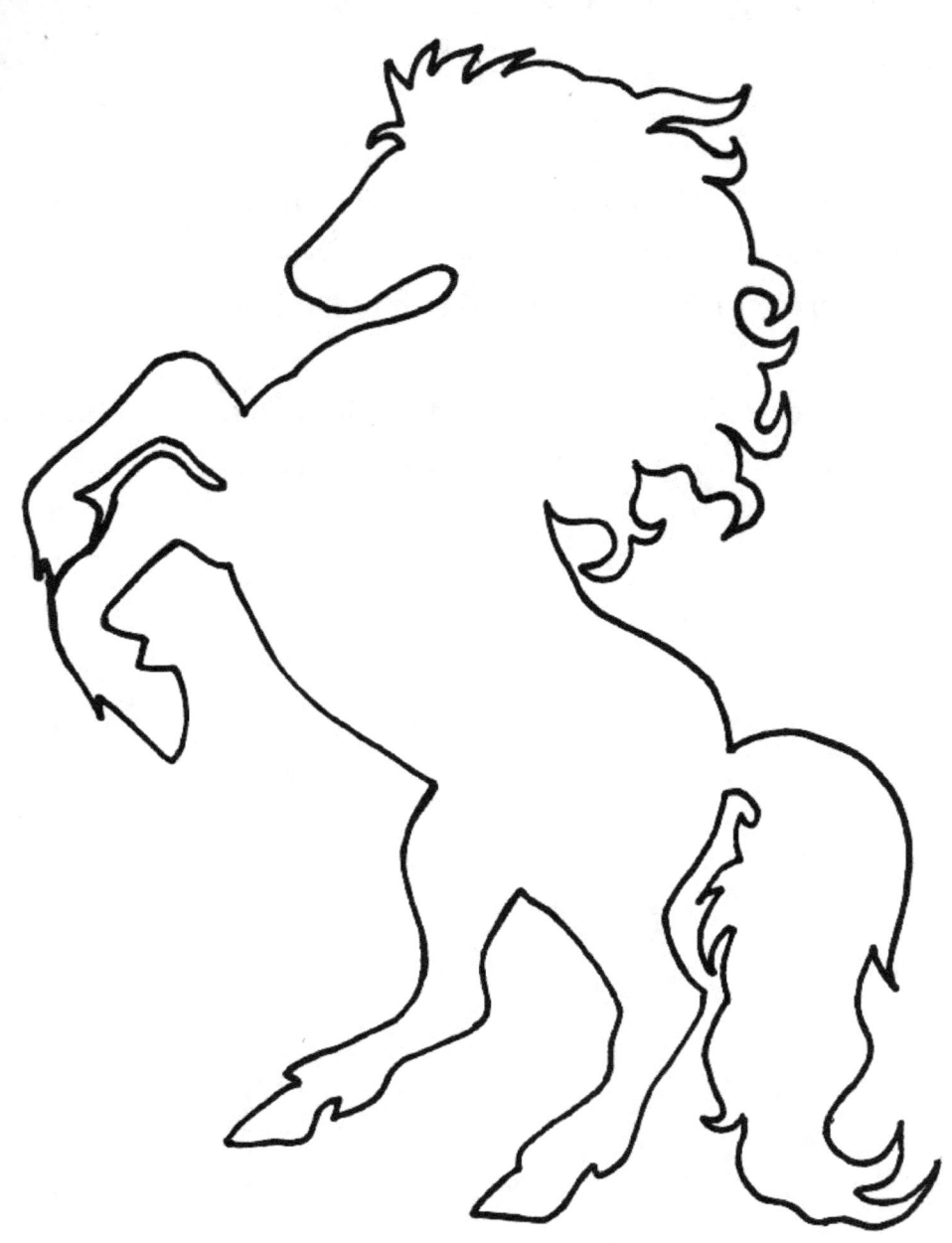

Step 2

Draw some swirls and leaves on the face and the mane of the horse. Embellish the swirls with some dots of different sizes along the curved lines of the swirls.

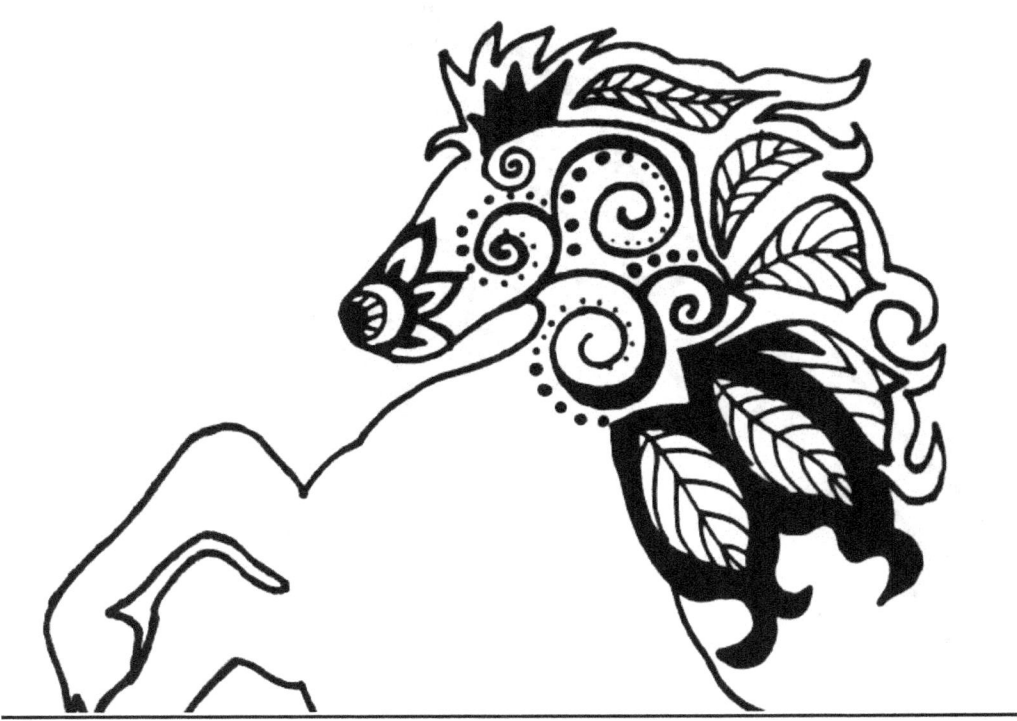

Step 3

Thicken the outlines of the leaves. This is done to place special emphasis on the mane.

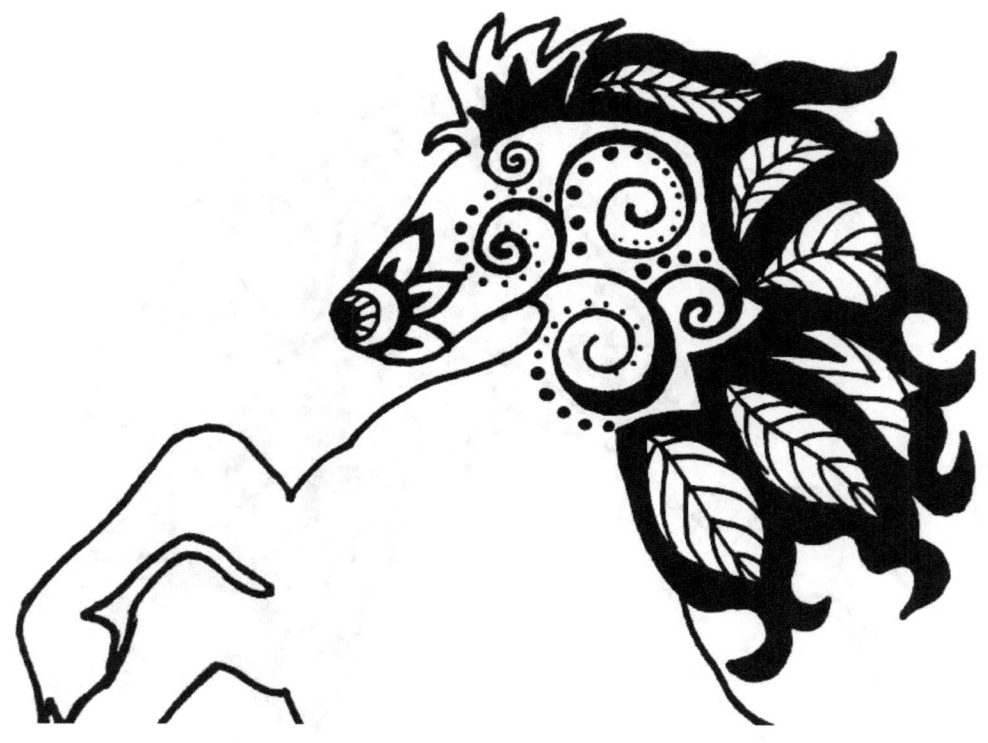

Step 4

Create the designs of decorative embellishments below the neck. The drawings shown in the illustration are made like the hangings used on festivals.

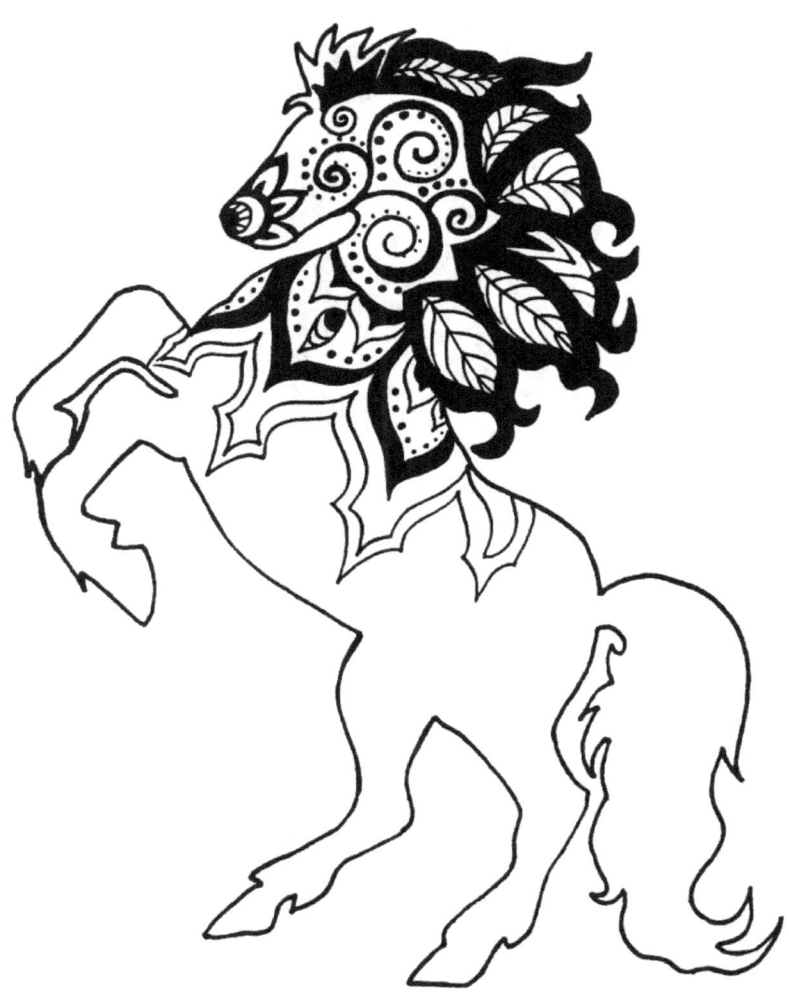

Step 5

Thicken the outlines of the drawings below the neck. Draw a chain starting from the fore-legs ending at the gaskin. You can take the inspiration for this chain from many things you see around you.

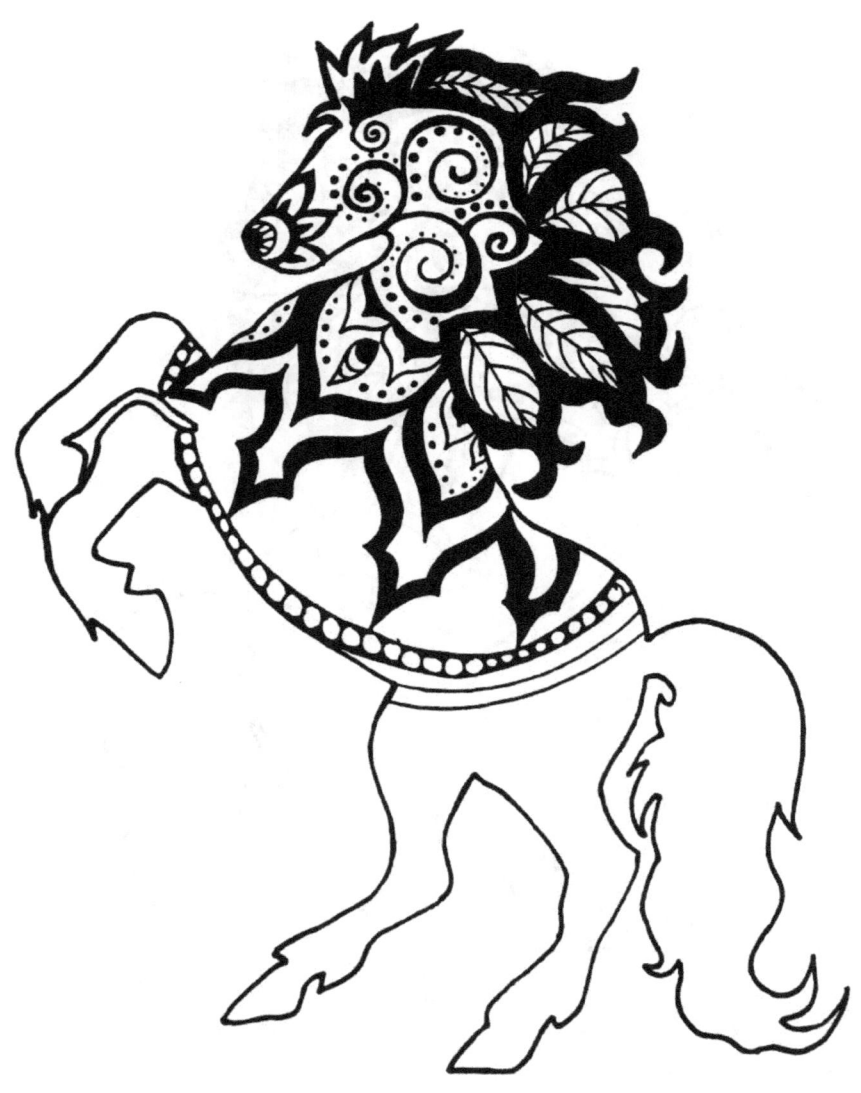

Step 6

The major part of the body of the horse is covered with the embellishments of festivities in our illustrations. But, you can take the liberty of drawing any kind of patterns you like. Use semi circles with dots at the joints of legs.

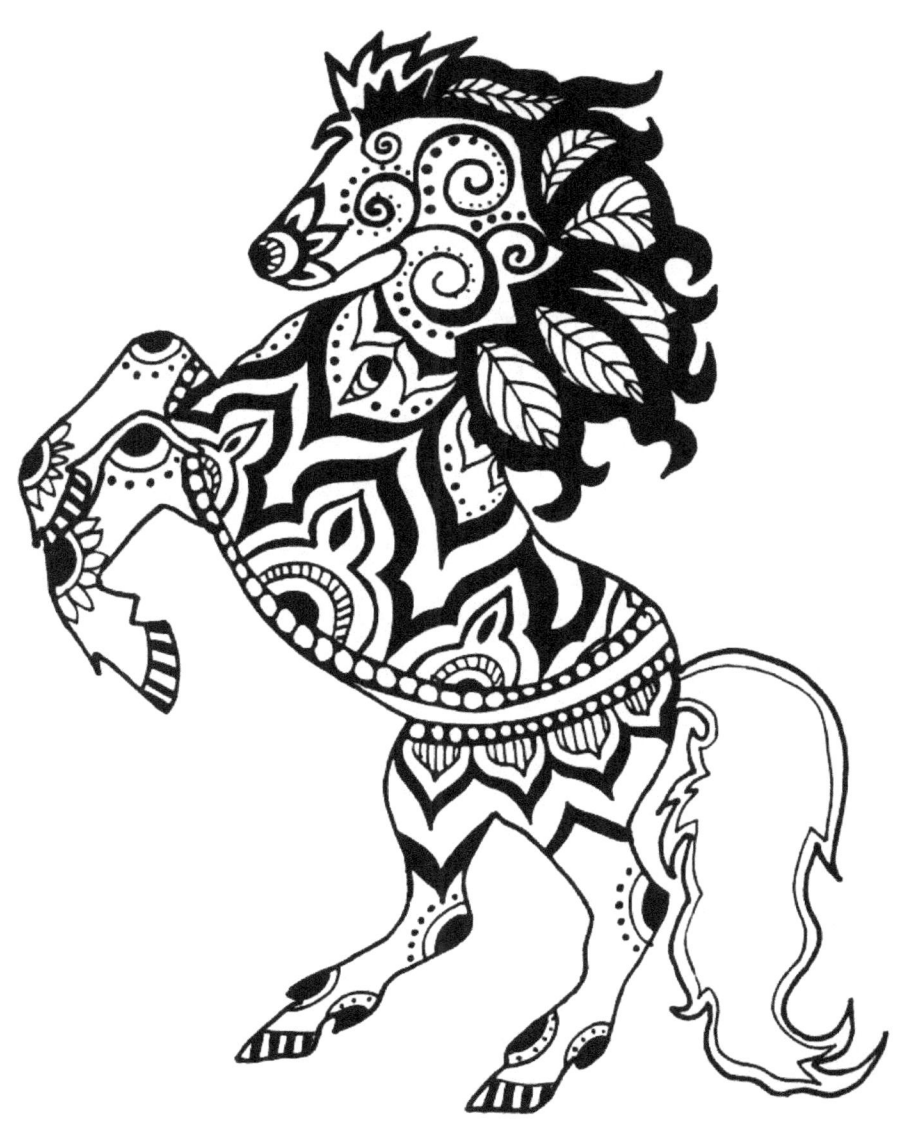

Step 7

Fill up the tail with flowers and dots of different shapes and sizes. You can also look at previous patterns of Zen Doodle for inspiration. Use stripes at the feet or hoof of the horse.

One more design of the Zen Doodle horse is complete.

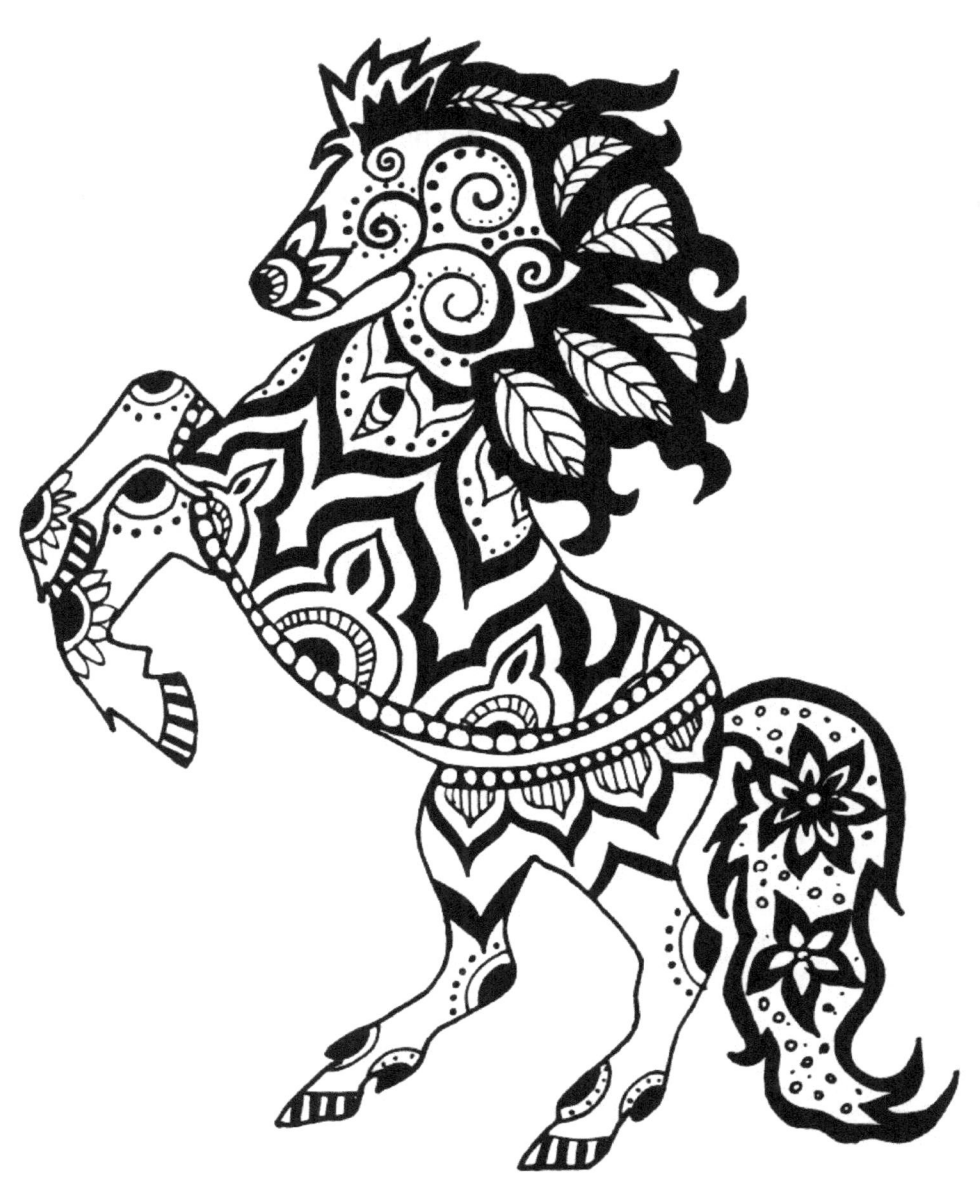

Chapter 4 - Horse Drawing 4

This horse is drawn unconventionally. We have just used the face and feet of the horse as inspiration. The rest of the drawing is based on the embellishments of different kinds.

You can also make any modifications to the design you are making.

Step 1

Draw the outline of the design you want to make. The flow of lines determines the quality of work in this design.

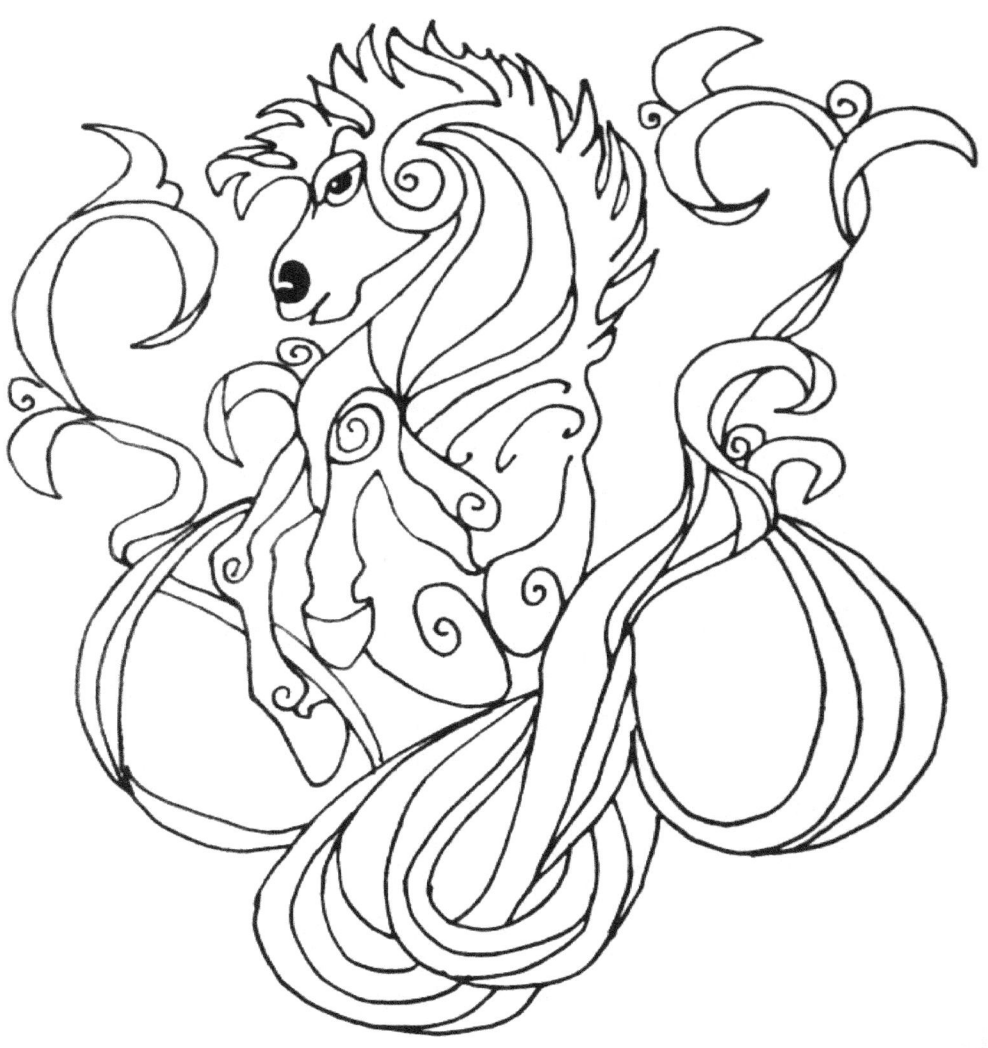

Step 2

Begin by filling embellishments in the portion of neck of the horse. You can use eye-like patterns in this area. Different swirls are also used in separate portions.

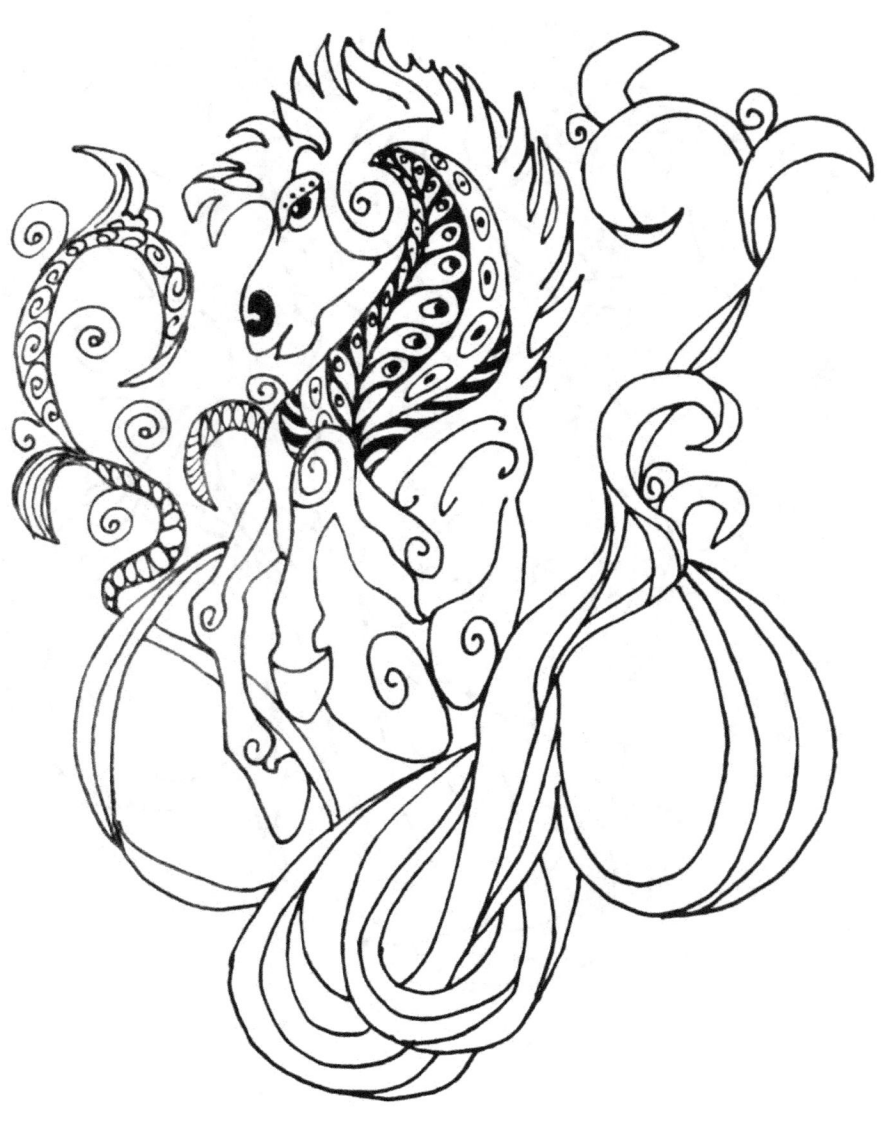

Step 3

Make the outlines of the mane bolder. The highlighted hairs of the mane look good in the finished design. Give a strip of triangles below the mane.

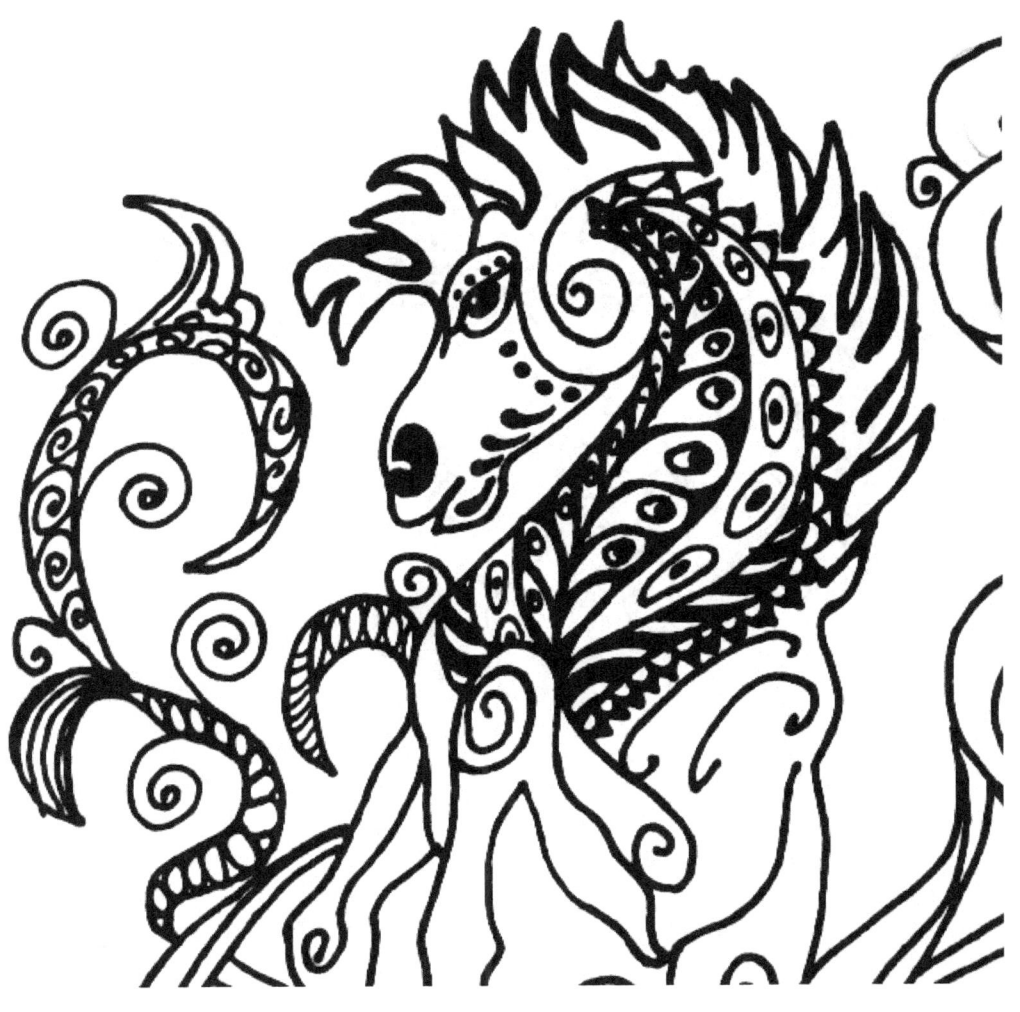

Step 4

Fill up some more area of the horse with checks, swirls, leaves, orbs and dots. You can also fill up the tail portion with striped pattern and thick zig-zag lines.

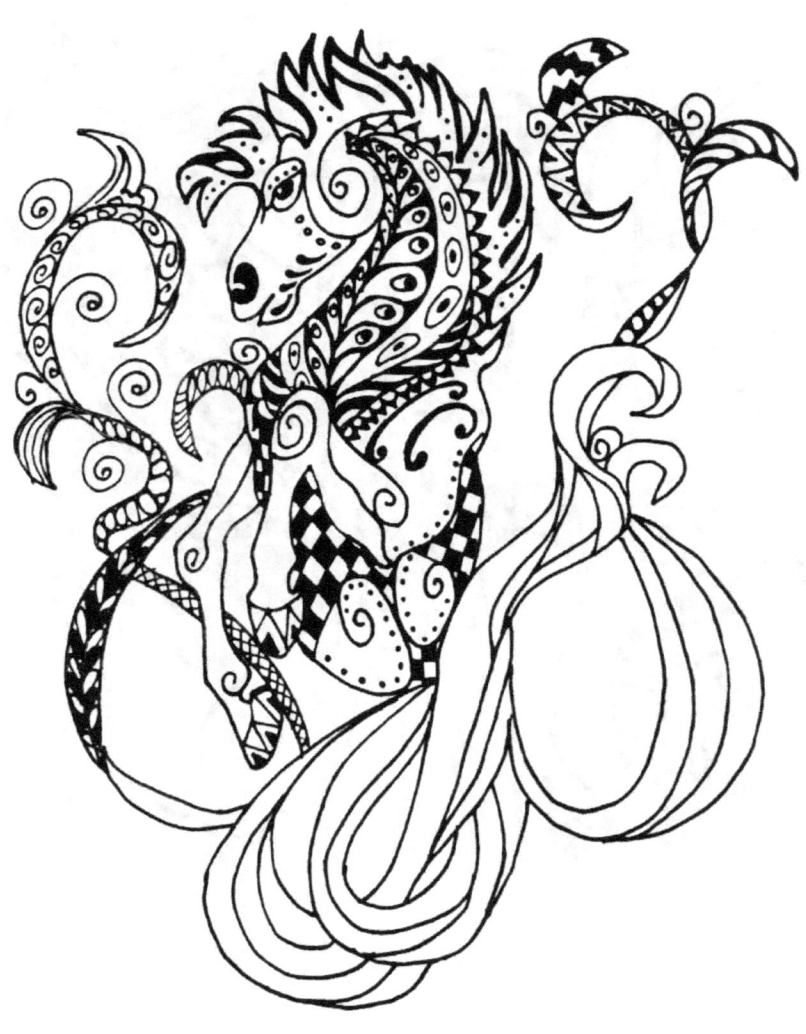

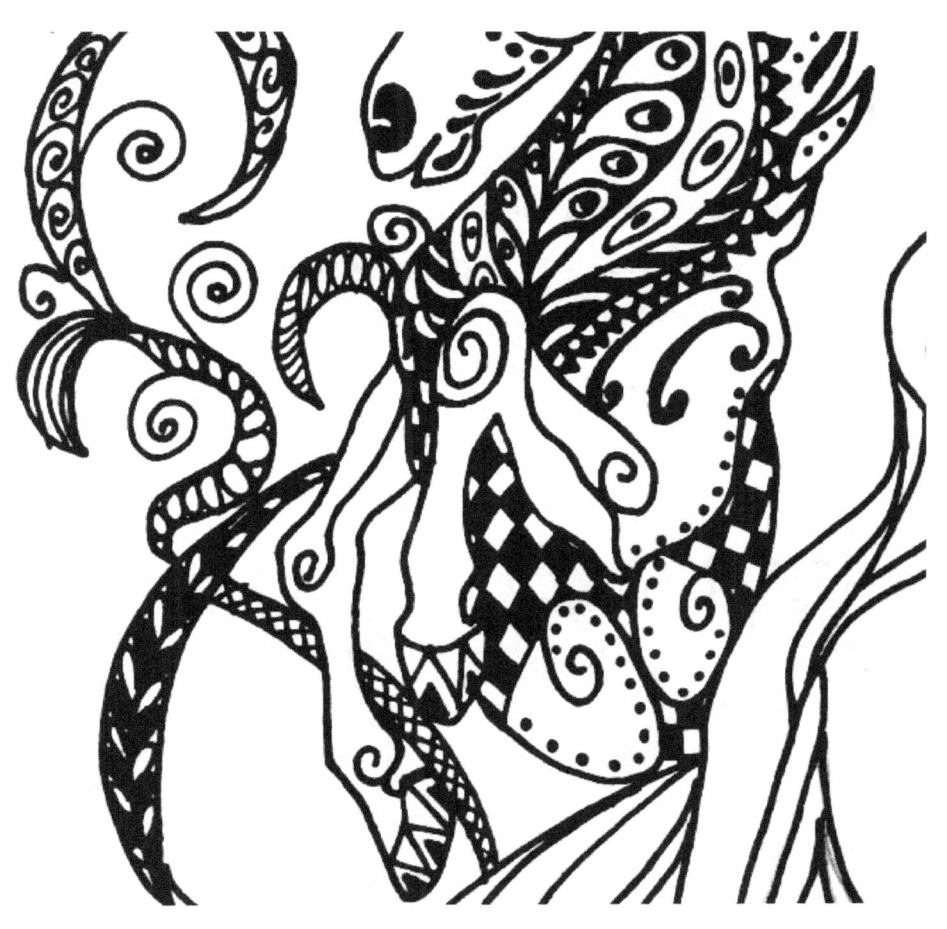

Step 5

The ribbons at the lower portion of the design are given tribal look by using thick zig-zag stripes. Triangles, circles, wires, dots and loops are used in different areas of the design to make it look intricate.

When all the areas are filled with various patterns, the Zen Doodle horse is complete.

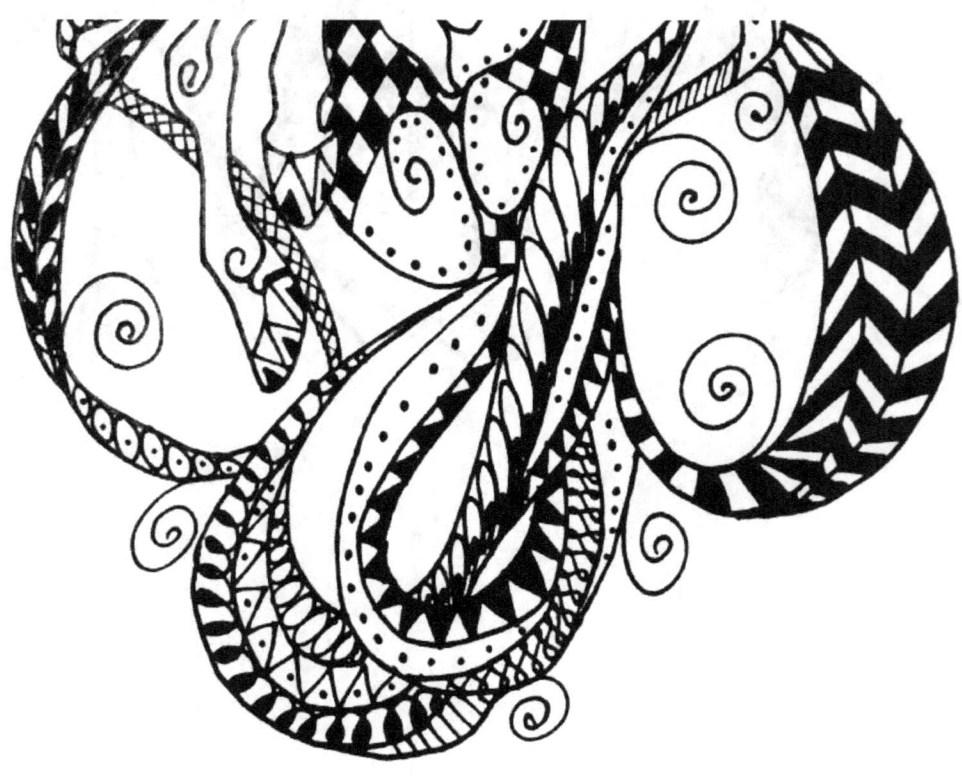

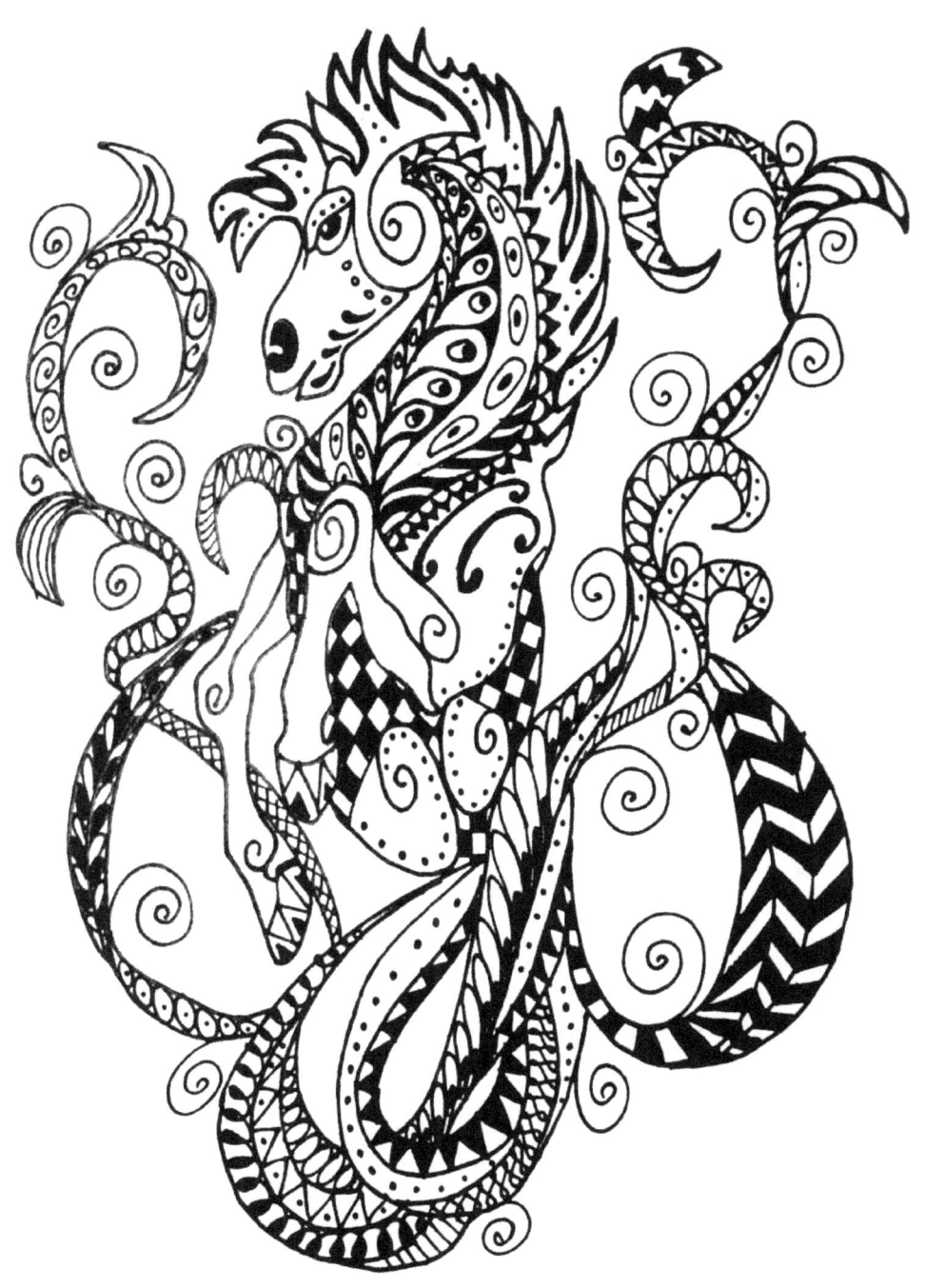

Chapter 5 - Horse Face

Step 1

Draw the outline of the face of a horse. A few floral strips have been drawn to give a natural look to the face. The mane is an important part of a horse. That is why; it is given special emphasis in every chapter. Here also, we have drawn the mane differently so that you can embellish it uniquely again.

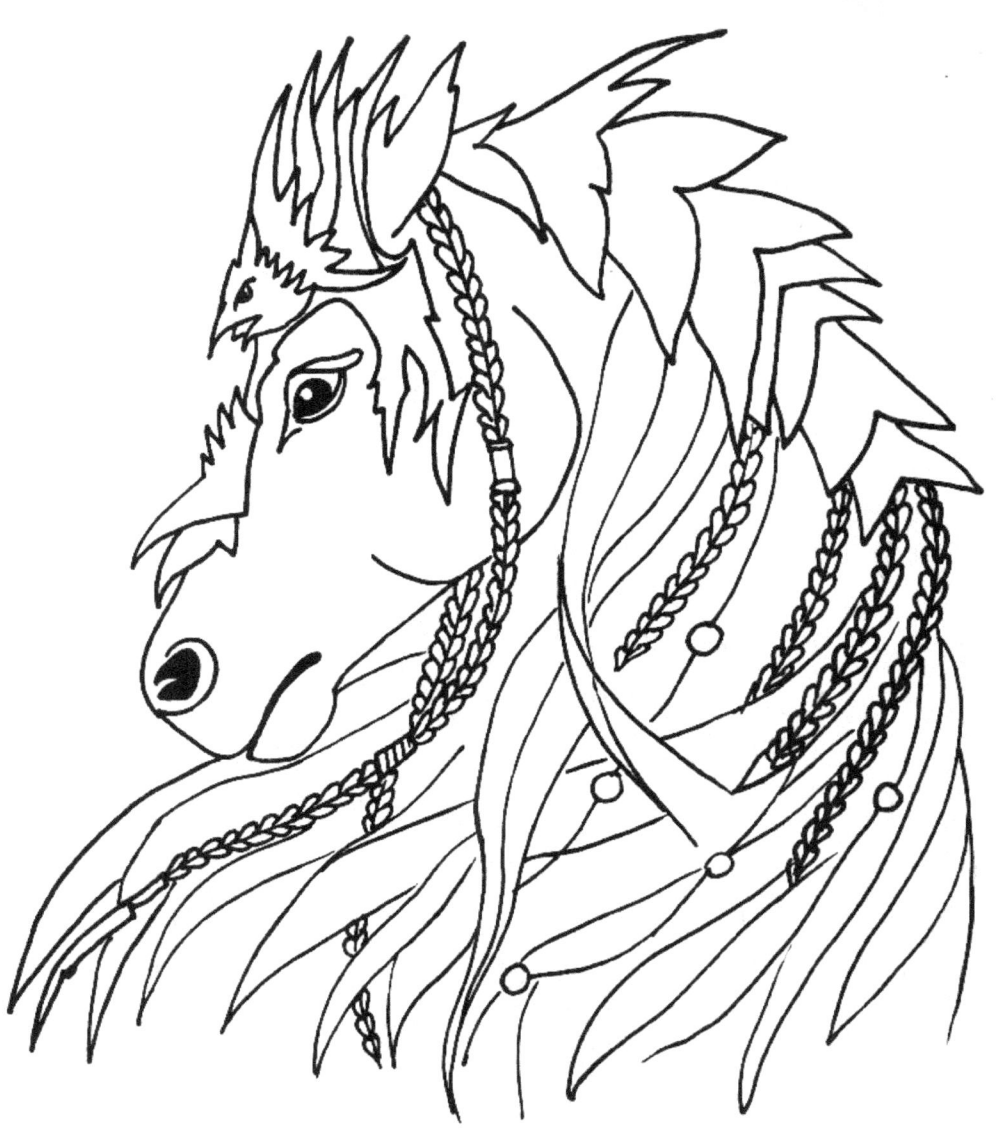

Step 2

Embellish the mane with patterns like orbs, leaves, triangles, semi-circles etc. The features of the face are given special emphasis here. Thus, draw the eyes, nose and mouth with precision.

Notice the beak of bird on top of the eye, which is placed like a crown on the head of the horse.

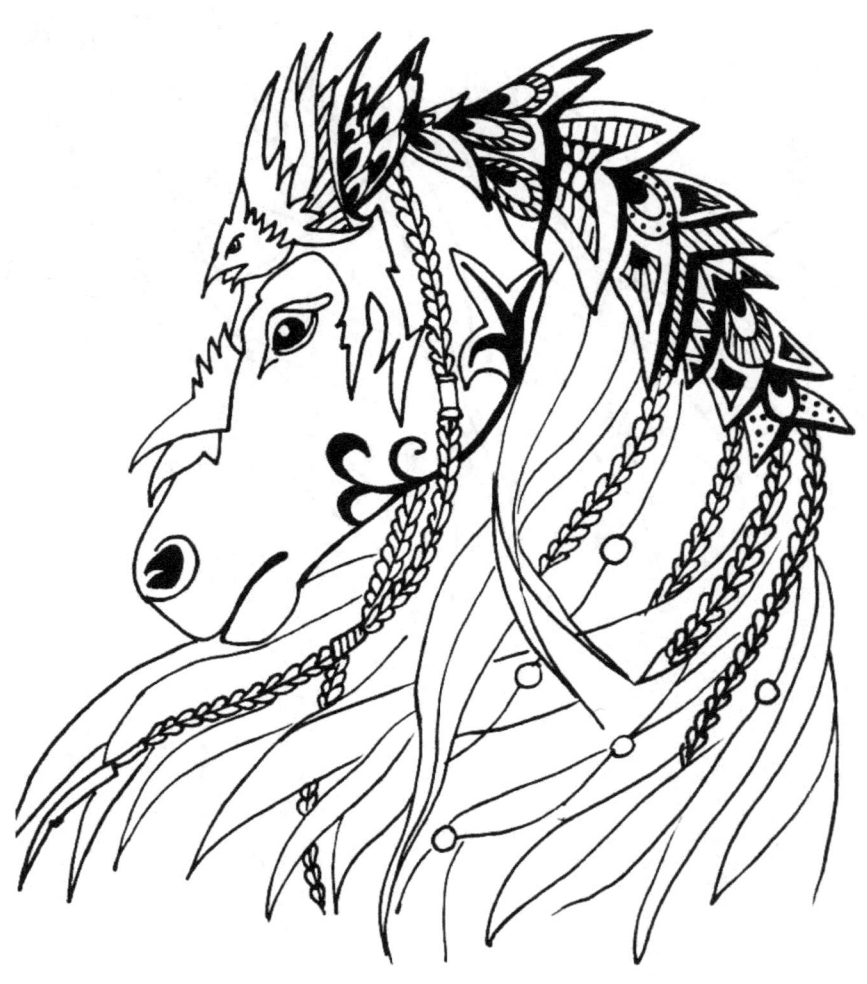

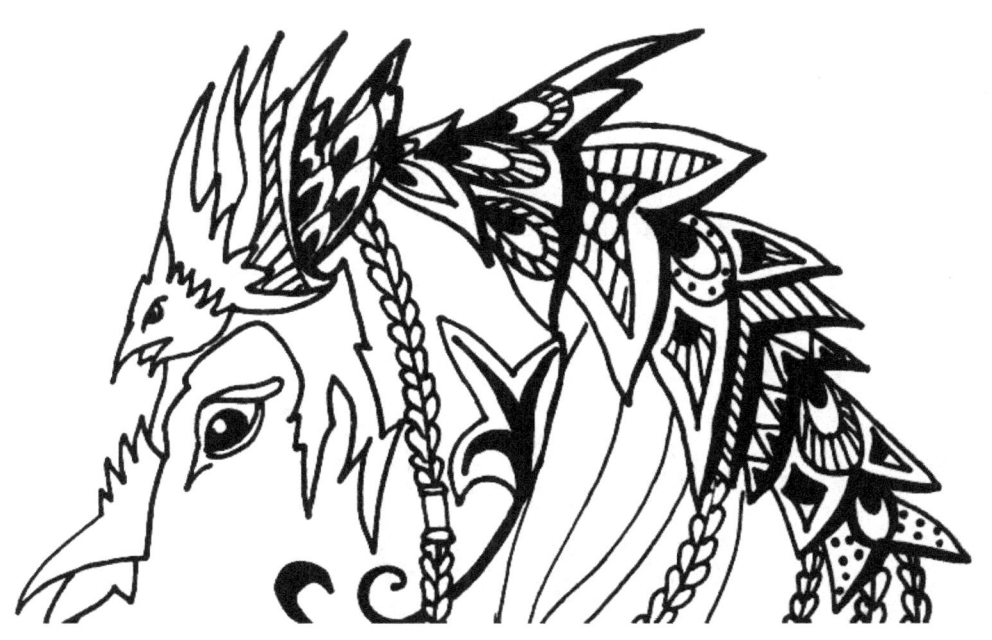

Step 3

Give freely flowing lines which symbolize the mane of the horse in the illustration. Use swirls, petals of flowers, dots, parallel lines to decorate the mane. A tri-branched swirl is beautifully placed near the mouth of the horse.

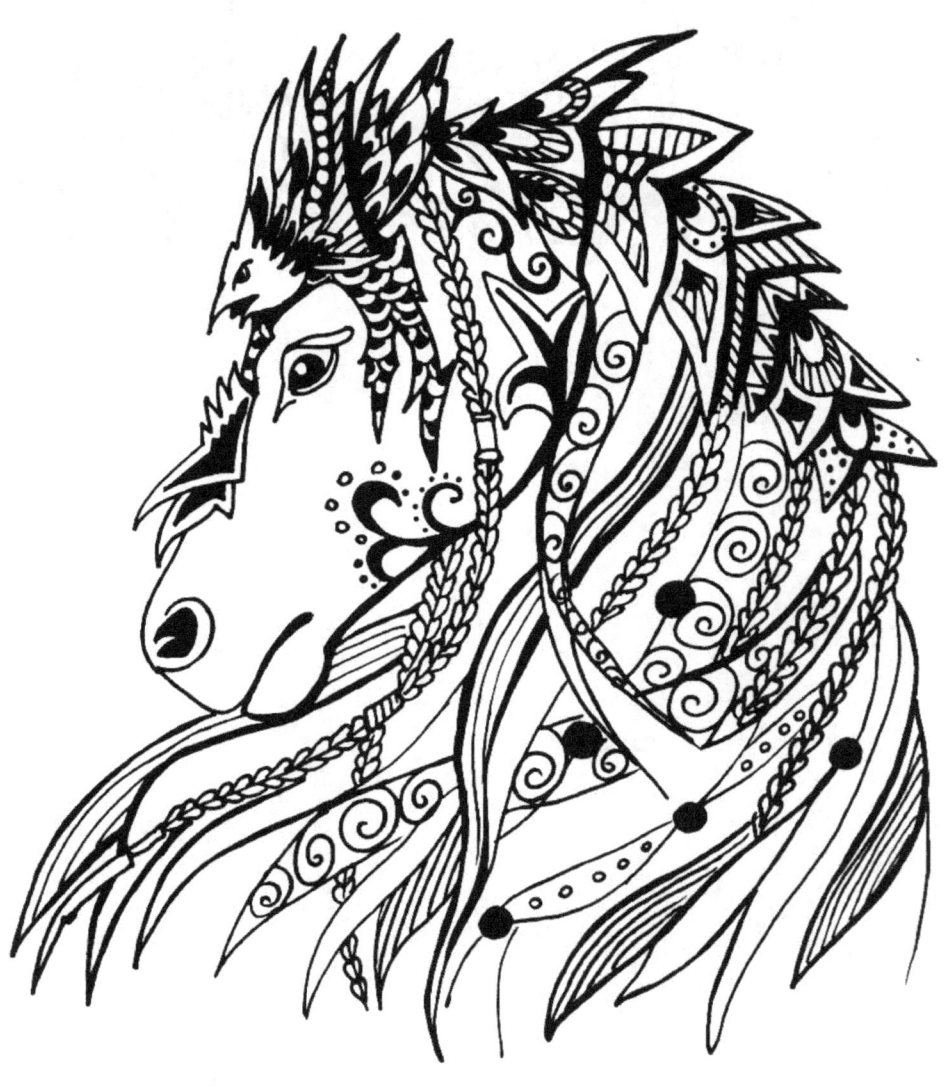

Step 4

Embellish the rest of the face and the mane using large and small swirls. The Zen Doodle face of the horse is complete.

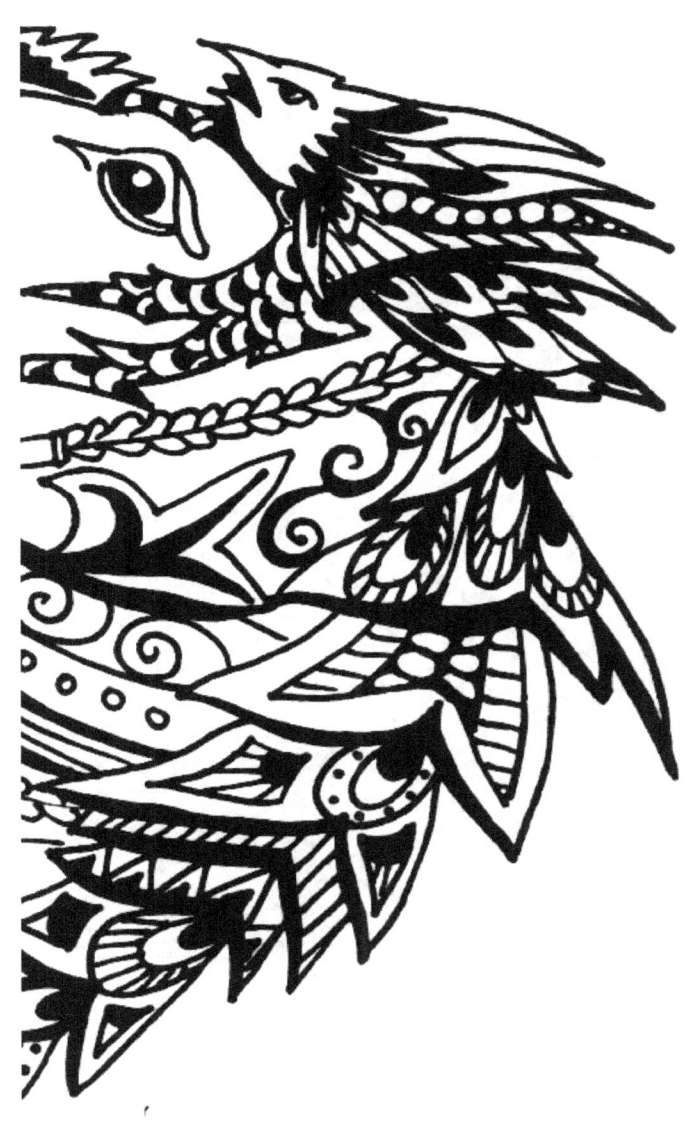

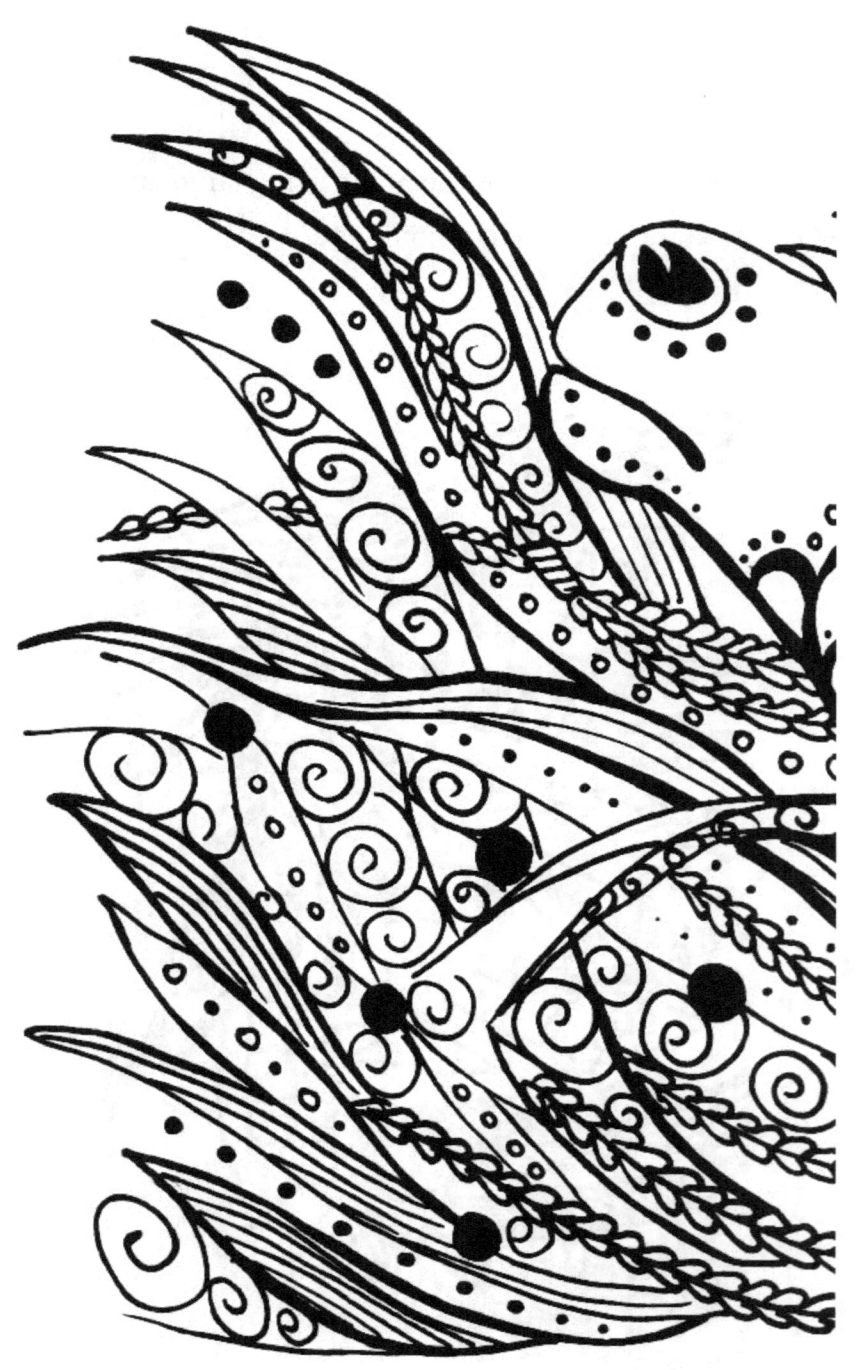

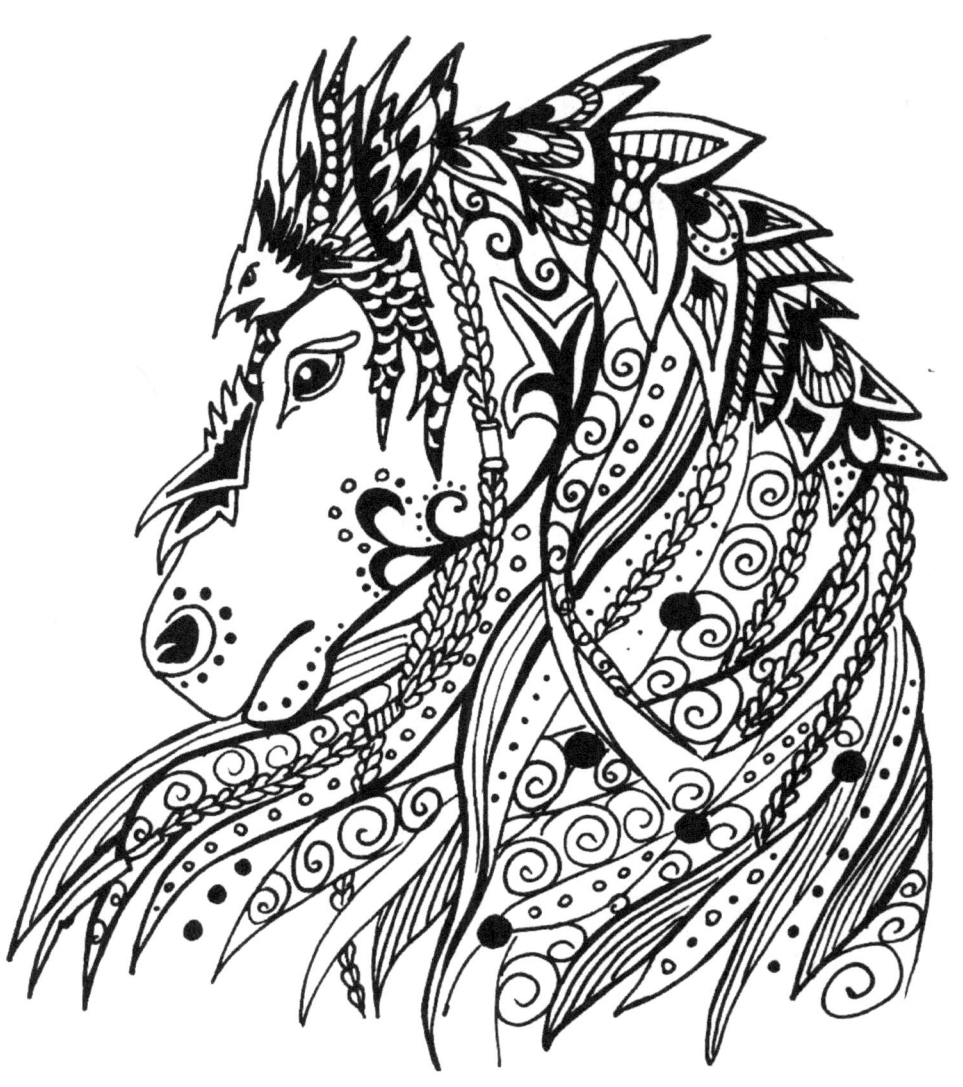

Chapter 6 - How to Take Inspiration from a Horse Face

The aim of this chapter is to teach you how you can see a picture and take instant inspiration from it. Here, we have taken inspiration from the face of a horse.

Step 1

Draw an outline of the horse face-inspired design. The free flowing lines are symbolic of the mane or the hair on the back of the neck of the horse.

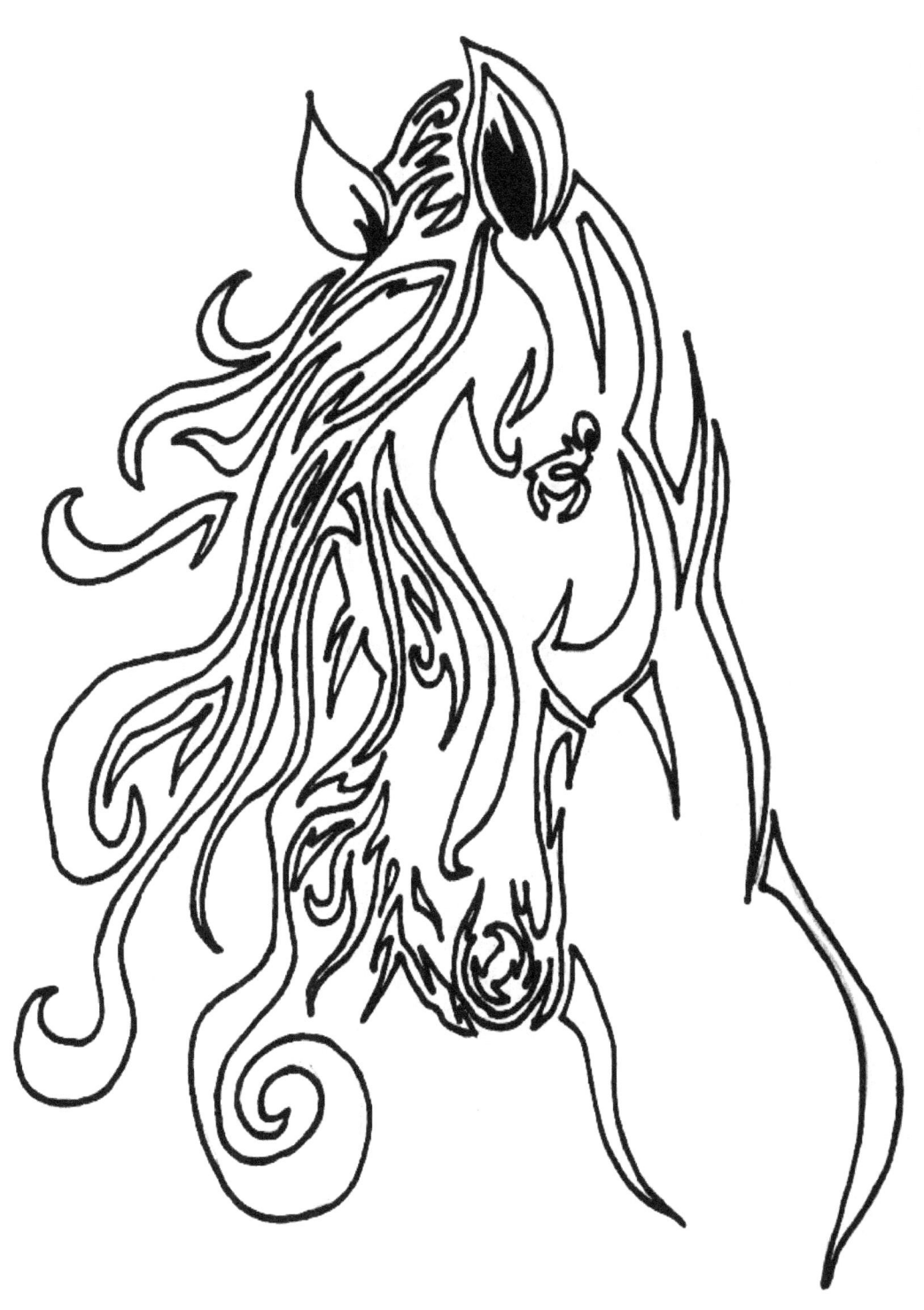

Step 2

Draw a long strip of eye-like figures in one of the major swirls. Draw other patterns like stripes, orbs, semi-circles etc in other strips.

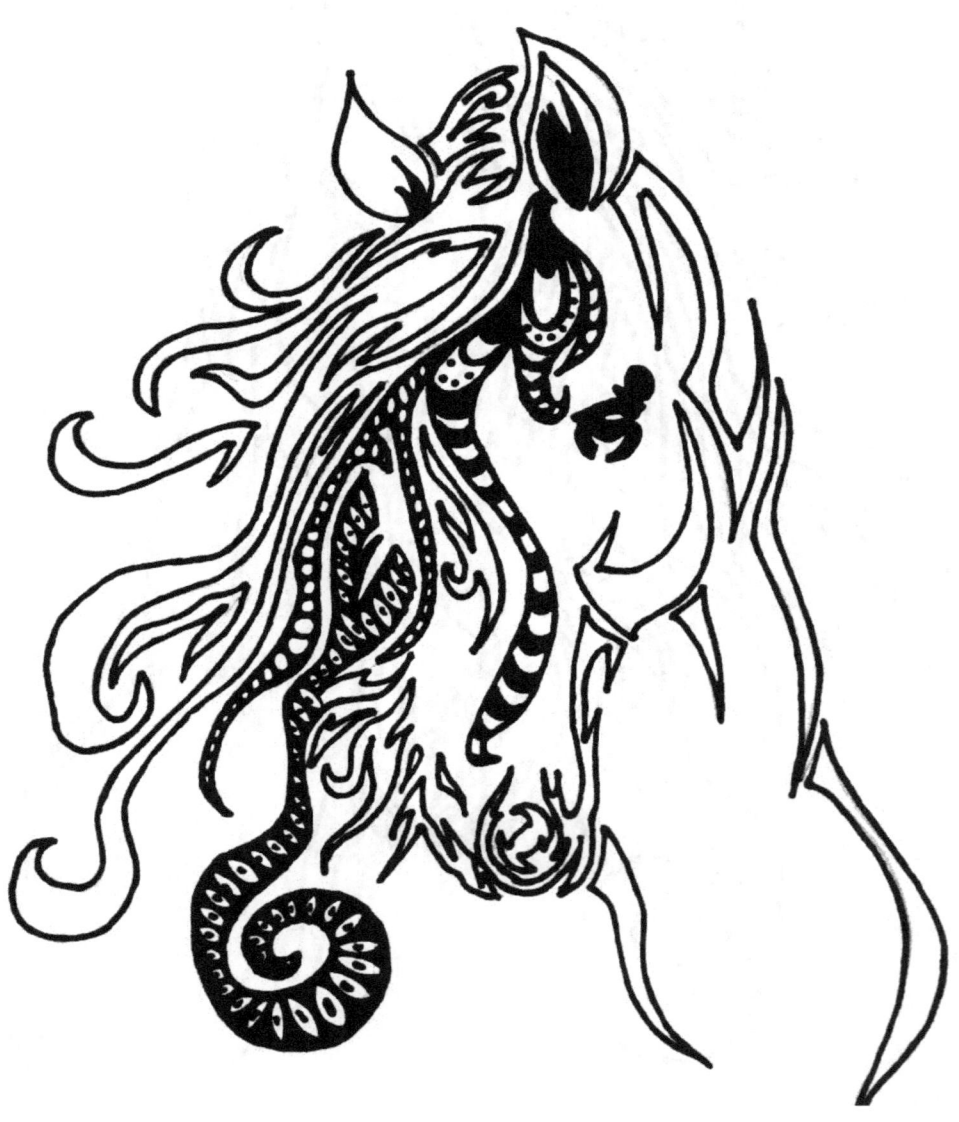

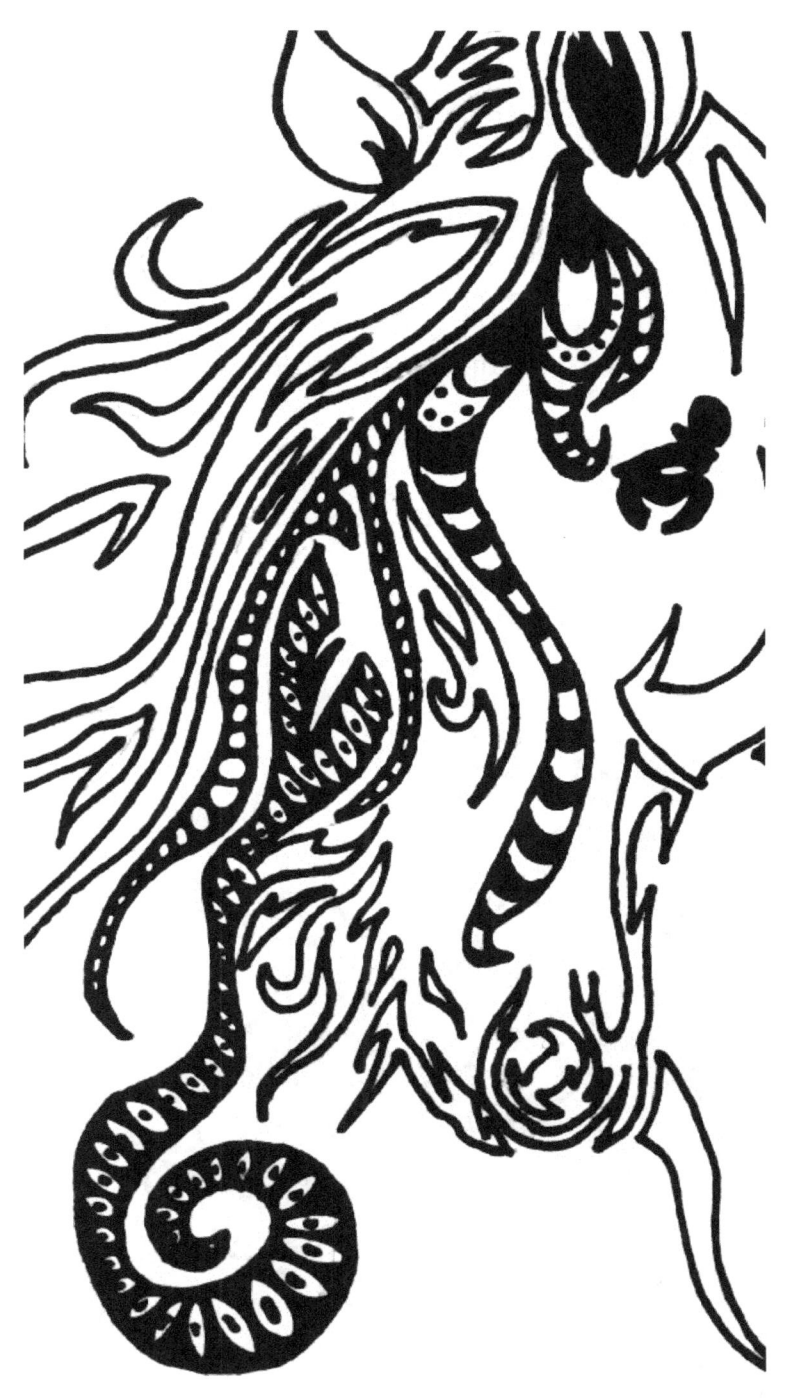

Step 3

Draw concentric circles with outlines filled with ink in one of the stripes on the left.

Basically, you just have to fill up the entire design gradually with different patterns.

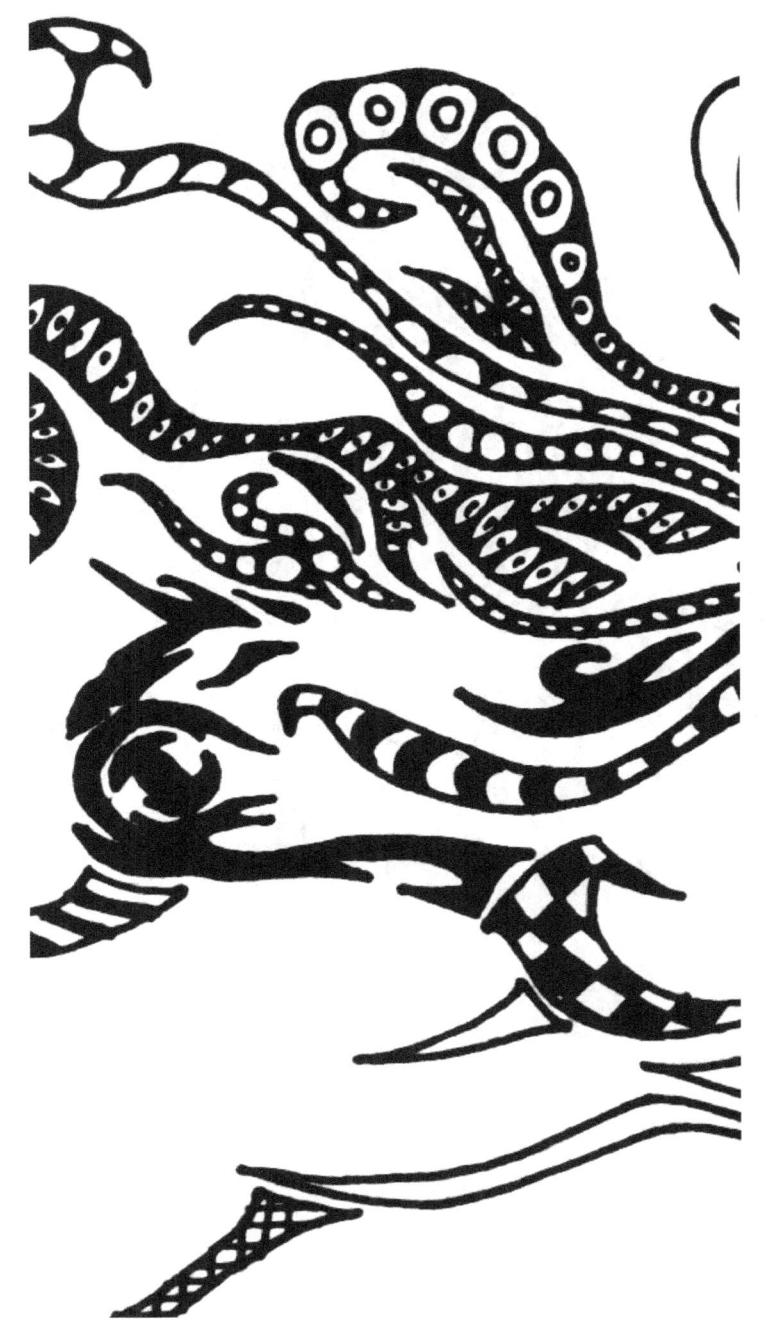

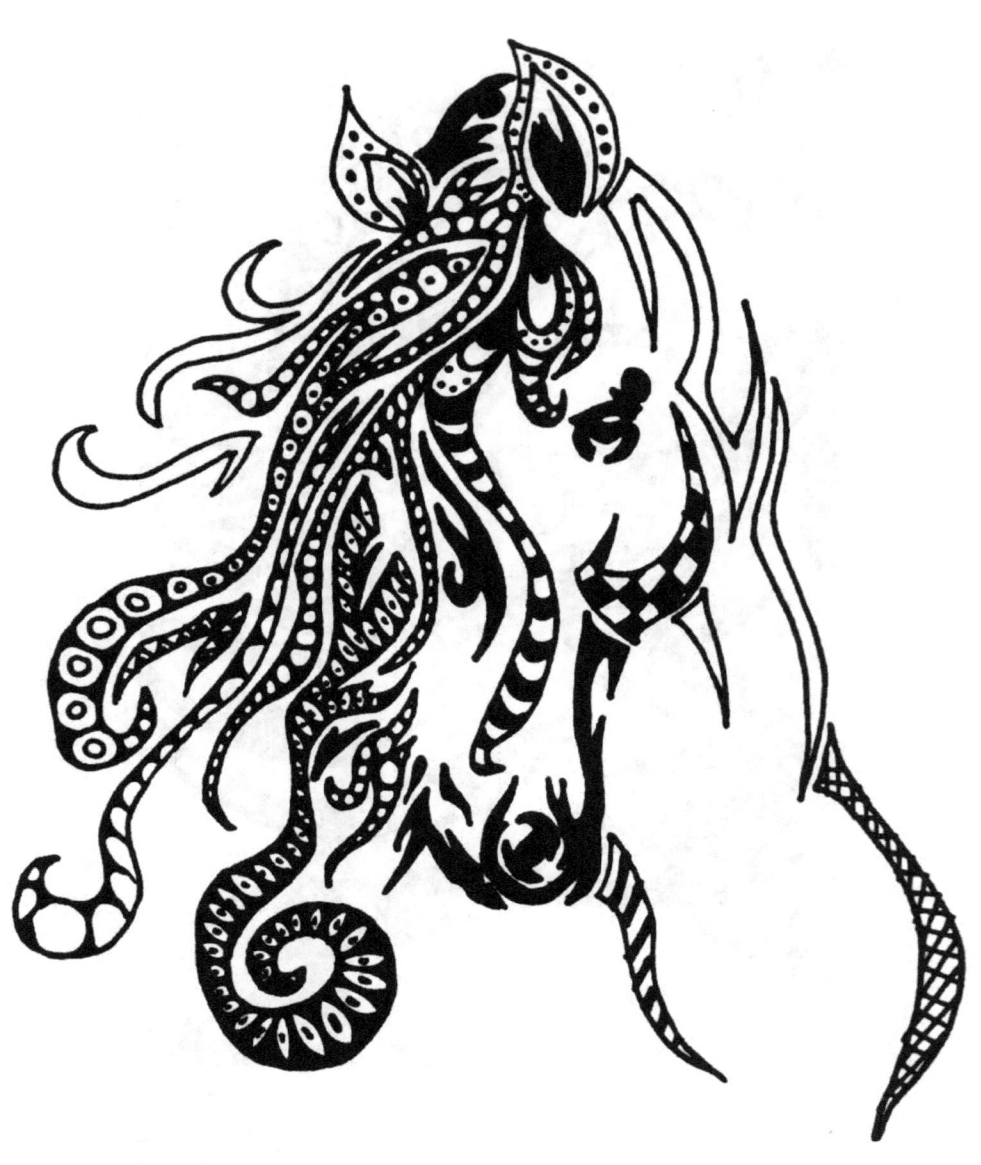

Step 4

Fill up the rest of the design with dots, checks, triangles, drops and thick lines. Highlight wherever you feel necessary.

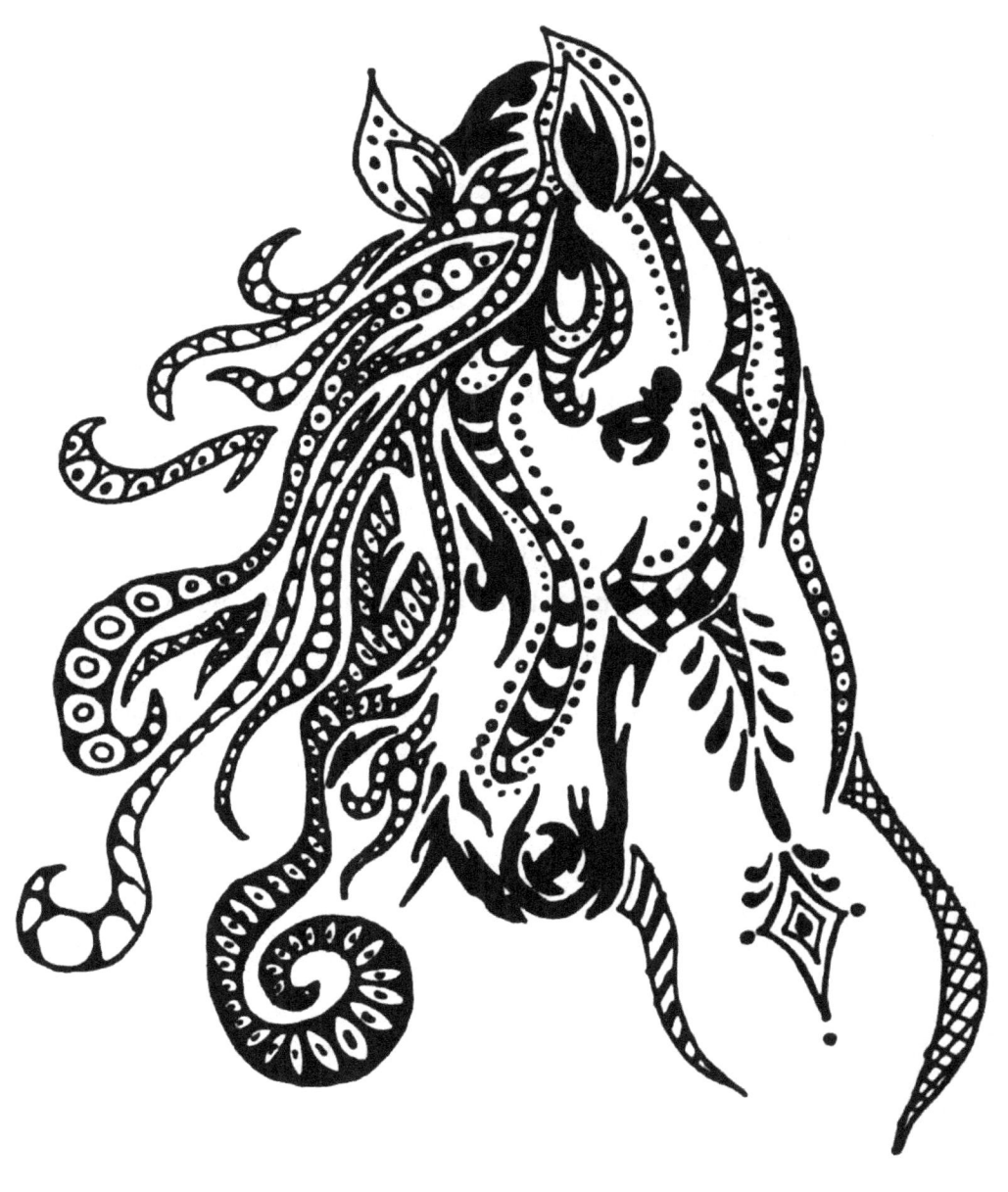

Conclusion

By now, you must have got the confidence to draw and explore the drawings in Zen Doodle genre of art. The concept of this section of art is not very difficult as it seems to be. People create enormous paintings using these tiny patterns only. Such artists treat Zen Doodle like mediation. They do not take it as a burden to create a painting.

Once you become comfortable to make drawings in this genre, you can also try your hands on a large canvas. If you move gradually, still you can finish a large painting in just one week. There is no need to get intimidated by the intricacy of the patterns. Even the largest of the works are made of the tiniest patterns. And as we have already mentioned before, you do not have to be an artist to master Zen Doodle. Thus, just forget the stigma attached to these beautiful drawings and get started to work.

Some patterns are already given in the illustrations. But, they are just the starting points of your drawings. They are given to facilitate the beginning process for you. You can explore many more designs on your own. You never know, you might be the next Zen Doodle expert writing blogs over the Internet. Keep practicing and you will definitely get the muse.
Good luck!

Thank you!

Thank you for choosing our book, we hope you found it interesting and helpful.

If you liked the book, please give us a favor to write your review.

We would really appreciate this!

If you would like to have a bonus – **FREE BOOK**, please send the screenshot of your review to this e-mail: **kelly.artbooks@gmail.com** and we will send you a **FREE BOOK** in PDF as a **GIFT!****

Hope to see you in our future books and good luck in your drawing experience!

** in the e-mail subject please mention the name of the book you reviewed and the author.

Other Books from Jane McKenty

ZEN DOODLE: The Art of Zen Doodle. Drawing Guide with Step by Step Instructions. Book one.

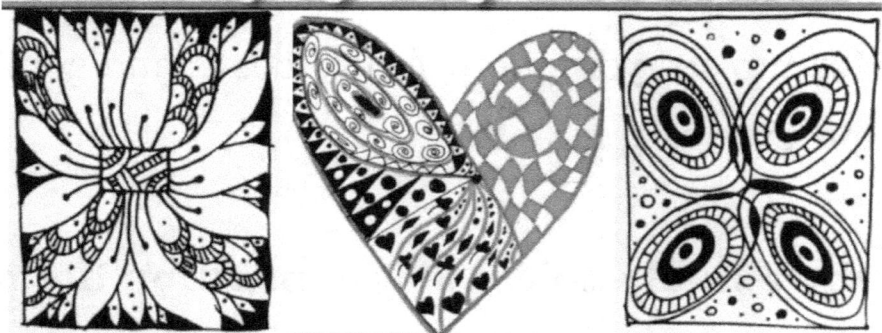

ZEN Doodle: The Art of Zen Drawing. Master Zen Doodle with Step by Step Instructions. Book two.

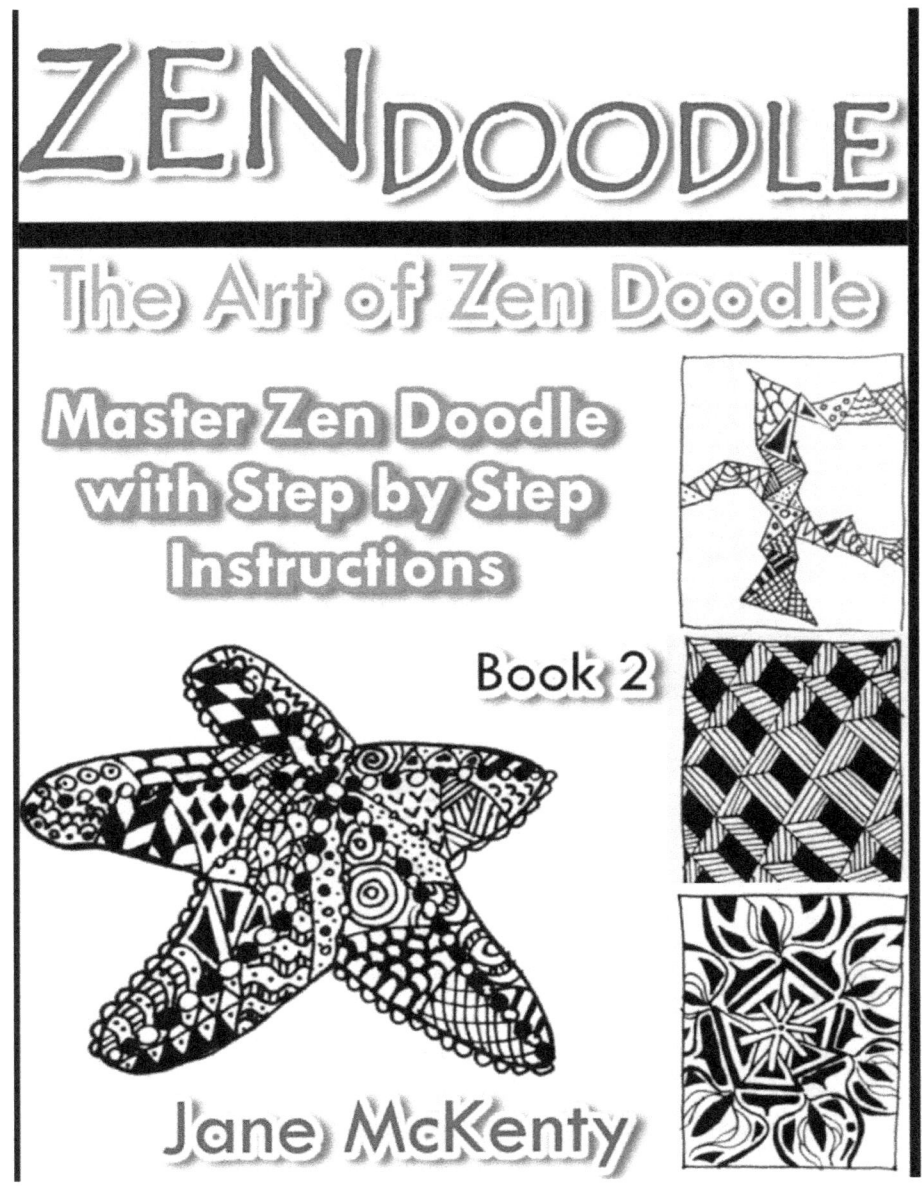

ZEN CATS: Drawing Amazing Zen Doodle Cats

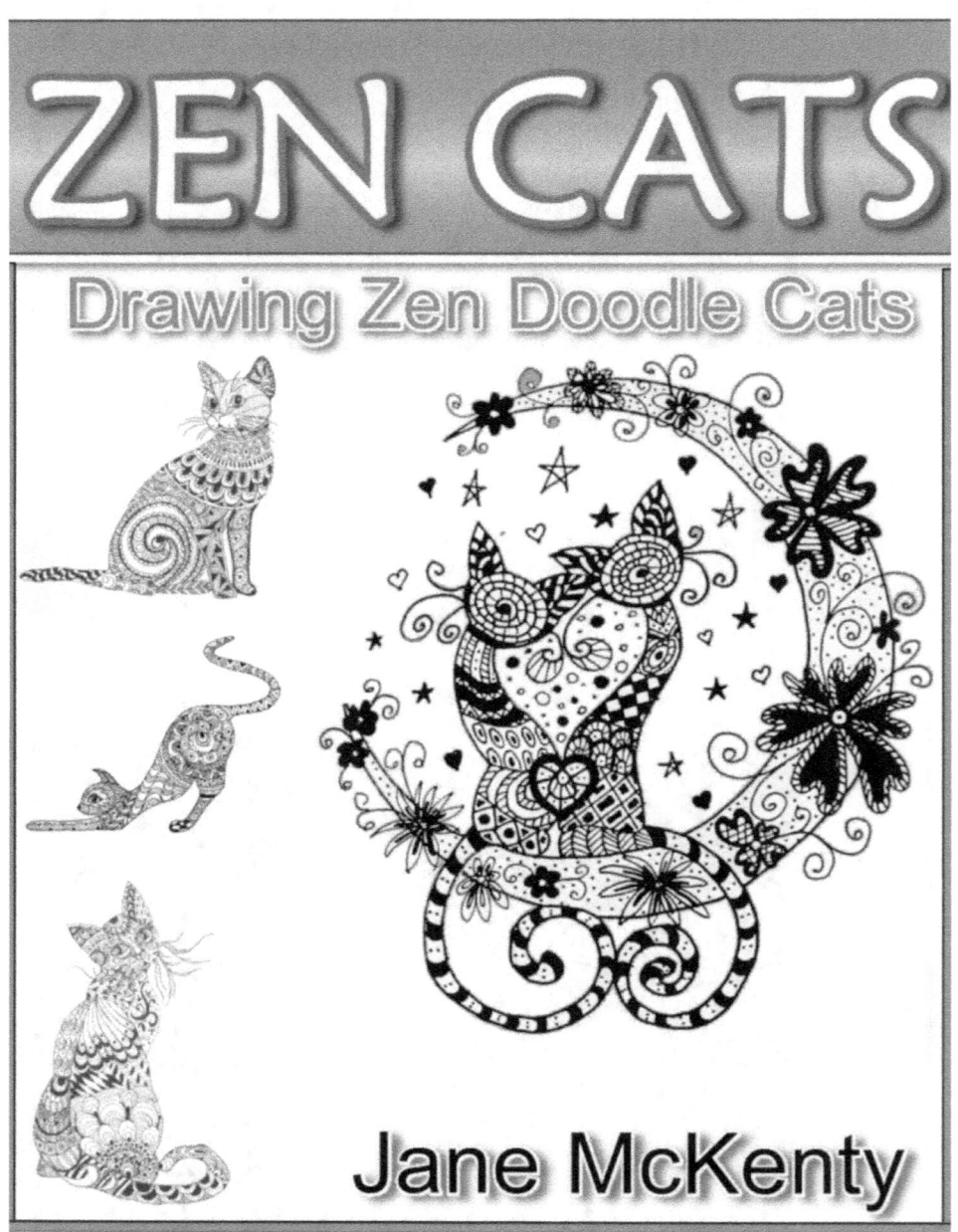

ZEN Girls: Drawing Amazing Zen Doodle Girls

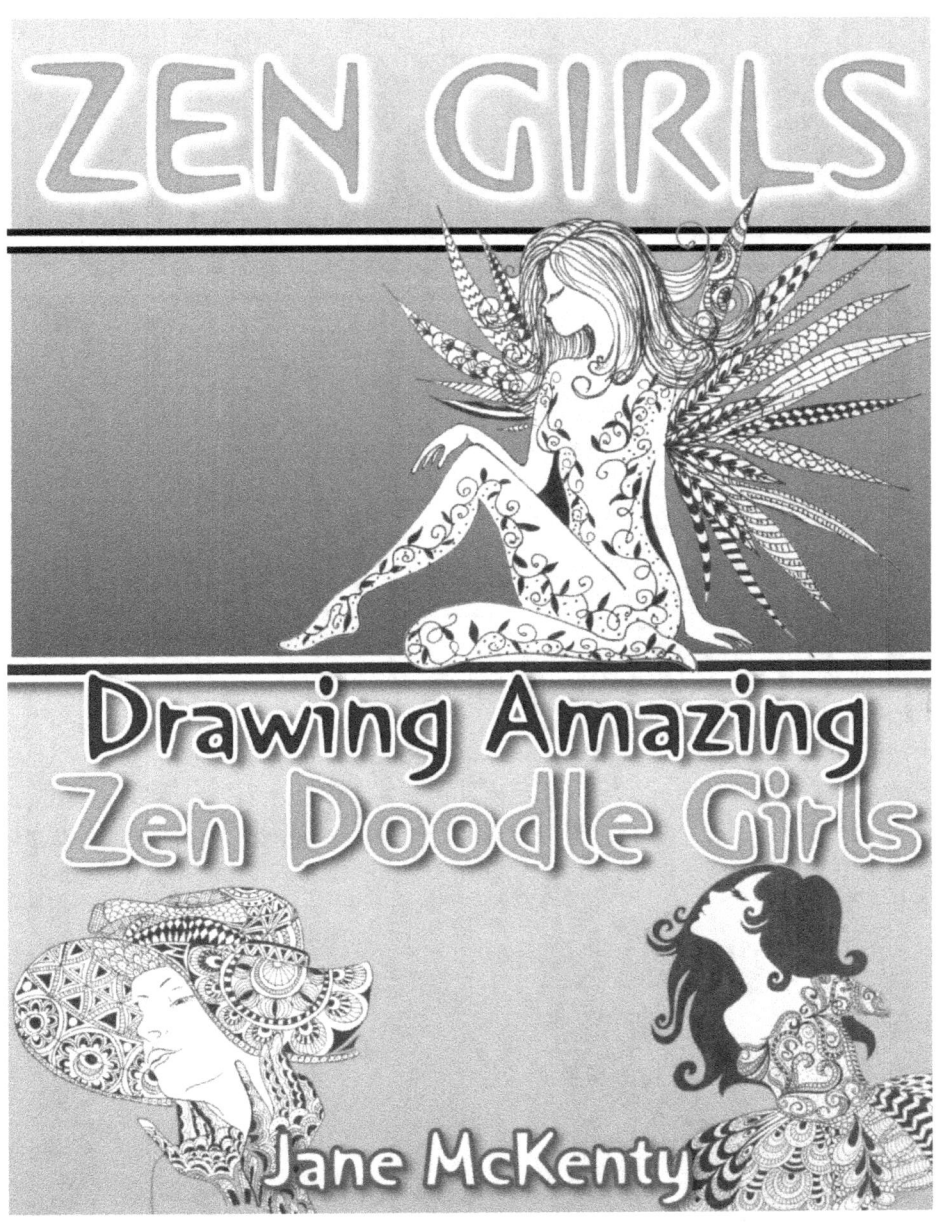

ZEN DOGS: Drawing Zen Doodle Dogs

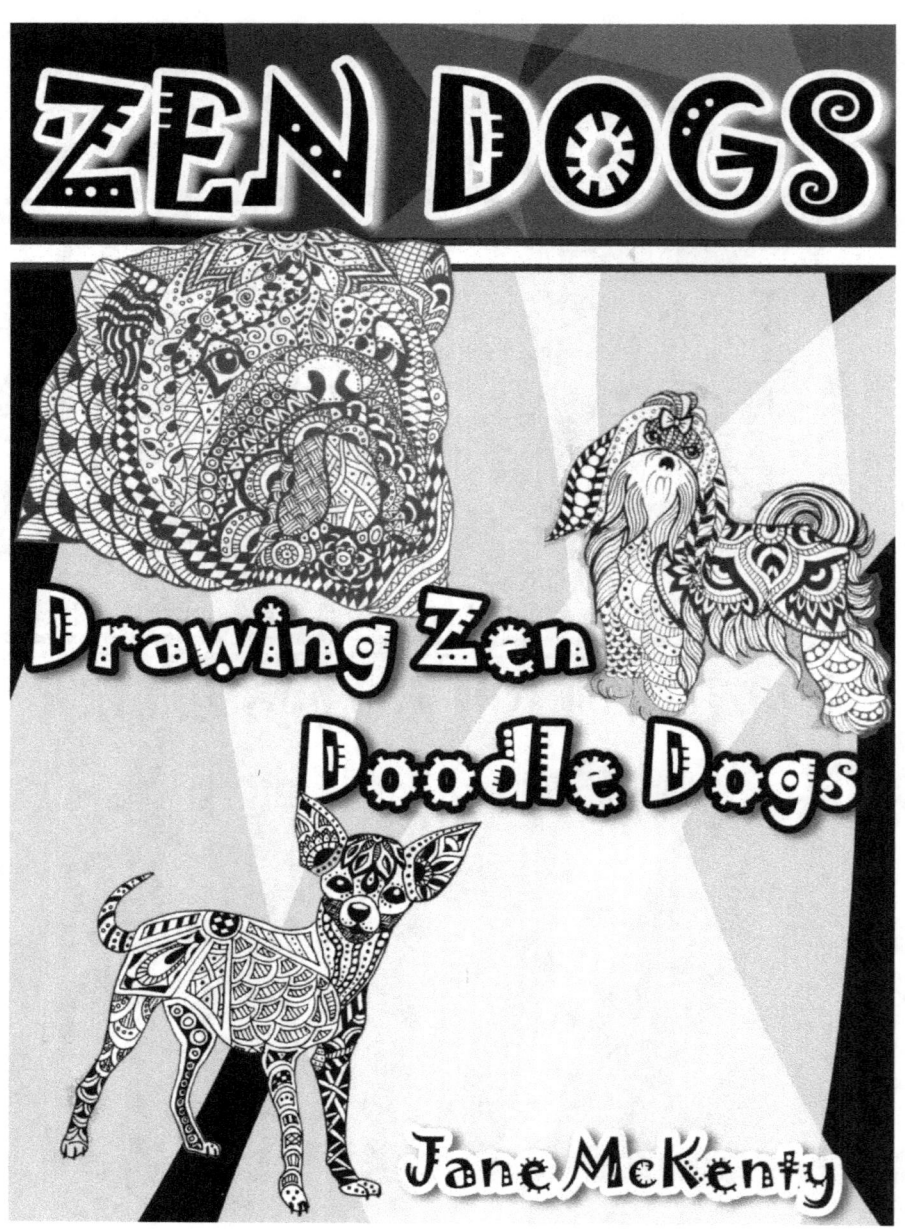

ZEN Doodle Art: Drawing Underwater Life with Amazing Zen Doodle Technique

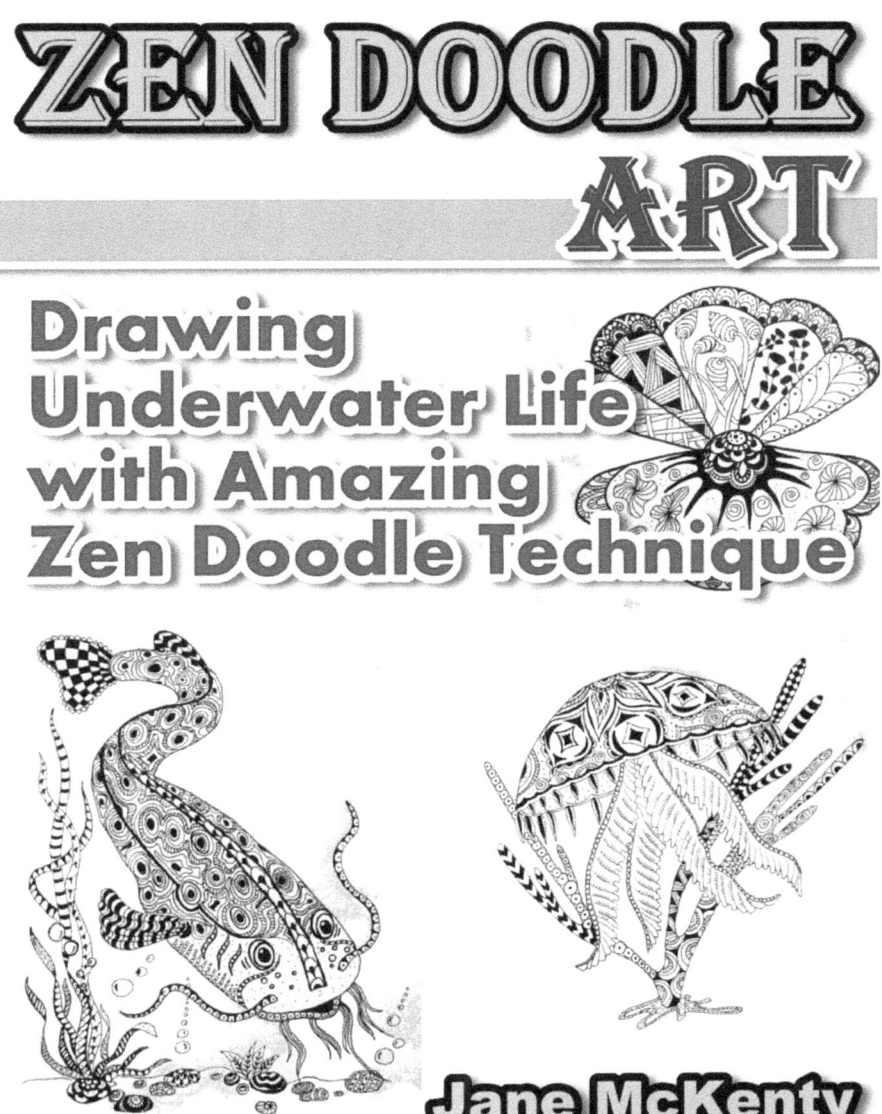